How to Have
Courage, Calmness,
and Confidence

How to Have Courage, Calmness, and Confidence

Paramhansa Yogananda

Crystal Clarity Publishers
Nevada City, California

Crystal Clarity Publishers, Nevada City, CA 95959
Copyright © 2010 by Hansa Trust
All rights reserved. Published 2012

ISBN: 978-1-56589-249-1
Printed in China
1 3 5 7 9 10 8 6 4 2

Created and produced by Crystal Clarity Publishers

Library of Congress Cataloging-in-Publication Data

Yogananda, Paramhansa, 1893-1952.
  How to Have Courage, Calmness, and Confidence / Paramhansa Yogananda.
    p. cm. — (The Wisdom of Yogananda ; vol. 5)
  Includes index.
  ISBN 978-1-56589-249-1 (tradepaper, illustrations)
  1. Courage. 2. Confidence. 3. Attitude (Psychology) 4. Yoga. I. Title. II.
Series.

  BF575.C8Y64 2010
  294.5'44 — dc22   2010003395

www.crystalclarity.com
clarity@crystalclarity.com
800-424-1055

Contents

Publisher's Note

Dear Reader,

Here is a handbook for reclaiming the highest power within you. Read this book carefully, absorb the power of the Master's words, practice his simple suggestions, and you will feel a new energy filling you, giving you the power to meet every challenge with joyful confidence, calmness, and courage.

Paramhansa Yogananda came to the United States from India in 1920, bringing to the West the teachings and techniques of Yoga, the ancient science of soul awakening. He was the first master of Yoga to make his home in the West, and his *Autobiography of a Yogi*, has become the bestselling autobiography of all time, introducing Westerners to their untapped soul potential.

Yoga is the ancient science of redirecting one's energies inward to produce spiritual awakening. In addition to bringing Americans the most practical and effective techniques of meditation, Yogananda showed how these principles can be applied to all areas of life.

The articles included in this book are taken from several sources: the lessons Yogananda wrote in the 1920s and 1930s, articles of his that appeared in *Inner Culture* and *East*

West magazines published before 1943, and the small book *Scientific Healing Affirmations*, published in 1924. Most of what is included here is not available elsewhere.

Crystal Clarity Publishers

How to Have
Courage, Calmness,
and Confidence

CHAPTER 1

COURAGE: AN INNATE QUALITY OF THE SOUL

Success, health, and wisdom are the natural attributes of the soul. Identification with weak thoughts and habits, and lack of concentration, perseverance, and courage are responsible for the misery that people suffer due to poverty, ill health, and so forth.

You are paralyzing your faculty for success by thoughts of fear. Success and perfection of mind and body are man's inherent qualities, because he is made in God's image. In order to be able to claim his birthright, however, he must first rid himself of the delusion of his own limitations.

God owns everything. Therefore, know at all times that as God's child you own everything that belongs to the Father. You must feel fully satisfied and contented, knowing that you have access to all your Father's possessions. Your native endowment is perfection and prosperity, but you choose to be imperfect and poor. The sense of possessing everything must be a mental habit with each individual.

⦿

Every day is a fresh opportunity on the part of the human ego to gather more and more exploits of heroism. Meet everybody and every circumstance on the battlefield of life with the courage of a hero and the smile of a conqueror. Whatever comes your way and needs attention must be considered a duty. Duty is not imposed upon man by any super-power. It is the inherent urge of life toward progression. Neglect of one's duty is a source of evil that can be avoided by wisdom.

Avoid associating with those who always complain about life. They may ruin your newly awakened spirituality, which is like a tender plant growing within you. Avoid such people and try to be happy always, no matter how you are situated. God will never reveal Himself to you unless you are contented and happy.

The true devotee banishes faint-heartedness. Resolutely he assembles a mental caravan of noble spiritual qualities, appointing Will Power and Devotion to the post of leadership, and sets out on his journey. He knows with unshakable faith that, once he frees his heart from every vestige of desire, he will attain true freedom at last. Onward, ever onward he travels, embracing high achievements on the way, but never allowing himself to become attached to any of them. Never does he rest until the end is reached. Such is the true devotee!

Change—even change for the better—is often approached with apprehension. "In giving up something," people think, "will I be left with nothing?" It takes courage to renounce the known for the unknown. It is not easy even to renounce a familiar pain for an unknown, and therefore uncertain, happiness. The mind is like a horse that for years has pulled its delivery wagon. The horse grows accustomed to its daily route, and cannot be convinced easily to walk a new one. The mind, too, will not lightly abandon its old habits, even when it knows they cause only misery.

Beneficial changes should be embraced with courage. As long as one's hopes for better things are opposed by fear of their attainment, the mind can never be at peace. Accept change, therefore, as life's only constant. Our lives are an endless procession of gains and losses, of joys and sorrows, of hopes and disappointments. At one moment we find ourselves threatened by the storms of trials; moments later, a silver lining brightens the gray clouds; then, suddenly, the skies are blue again.

☙

The sincere seeker, in contrast to the armchair "seeker" who wastes his life spinning intellectual theories, takes heart at the thought of the hard work before him. A true warrior, though afraid, plunges courageously into battle when the strength of his arm is needed. A true alpinist, though apprehensive of the sheer cliff he faces, sets out resolutely to conquer it. And the sincere truth seeker tells himself, "I know what an arduous task it must be to achieve perfection, but I will give it all I have. With God's help, success, surely, must be mine!" By deep, daily efforts in meditation he conquers flesh-consciousness at last, and regains his long-lost awareness of the divine bliss within.

O devotee, take heart! No matter how dry, clay-hard, and cracked the soil of your heart has become during famine years of sense indulgence, of failure and disappointment, it can be watered and softened again by peace-showers of inner communion. Your spiritual enthusiasm, long wilted, can be revived. Only drink once more the ancient wine of God communion. In the field of fervent spiritual endeavor, as, daily, you work the softened soil of renewed soul-perceptions, sow once again the seeds of spiritual success, and watch them grow into a new crop of divine joy.

Instead of being overcome and discouraged when confronted with what you think is trouble, thank the Father for offering you the opportunity to see what you need to learn and to develop the strength and wisdom to meet the challenge.

⁂

Karma is best worked out by meeting life's tests cheerfully and courageously. If you still fear something, that karma has not yet been worked out. To dissipate it, don't try to avoid the tests you have to face. Rise above them bravely, by dwelling in God's joy within.

⁂

At any given moment you have all the courage, strength, and intelligence necessary to overcome any seeming difficulty. Become still, mentally and physically. Retire to your center of poise within, and commune with your Father there. He will show you the way.

⁂

Affirmations for Courage

I will seek safety first, last, and all the time in the constant inner thought of God-peace.

I will wipe the dream fears of disease, sadness, and ignorance from the soul's face of silence, with the veil of Divine Mother's peace.

I am protected behind the battlements of my good conscience. I have burned my past darkness. I am interested only in today.

There is a right solution to every problem. I have within me the wisdom and intelligence to see this solution, and the courage and energy to carry it through.

God is within me and around me, protecting me, so I banish the gloom of fear that shuts out His guiding light and makes me stumble into ditches of error.

Secret fear creates tension and anxiety, and brings ultimate collapse. We must have faith in our ability, and hope in the triumph of a righteous cause. If we do not possess these qualities, we must create them in our own mind through concentration. This can be accomplished by determined and long-continued practice.

First, we must identify our defects. If, for example, we are lacking in will power, let us meditate upon it, and through conscious effort we shall be able to create strong will power in ourselves.

If we want to relieve ourselves of fear, we should meditate upon courage, and in due time we shall be freed from the bondage of fear. Through concentration and meditation, we make ourselves powerful and able to focus our attention. Continual practice will enable us to concentrate our energy upon a single problem or a single responsibility without any effort. It will become second nature to us. Possessed with this new quality, we shall succeed in our life's undertakings, both spiritual and material.

※

Sorrow has no objective existence. If you constantly affirm it, it exists. Deny it in your mind, and it will exist no longer. This is what I call the hero in man: his divine or essential nature. In order to acquire freedom from sorrow, man must assert his heroic Self in his daily activities.

The root of sorrow lies in the dearth of heroism and courage in the normal man. When the heroic element is lacking in the mental make-up of a person, his mind becomes amenable to all passing sorrows. Mental conquest brings happiness into life, and mental defeat brings sorrow. As long as the conqueror in man is awake, no sorrow can shadow the threshold of his heart.

Tears and sighs on the battlefield of life are the liquid cowardice of a weak mind. Those who give up the fight become prisoners within the walls of their own ignorance. Life is nothing if not a continuous overcoming of problems. Every problem that waits for a solution at your hand is the religious duty imposed upon you by life itself.

There can be no life that is not full of problems. Essentially, conditions are neither good nor bad; they are always neutral, seeming to be either depressing or encouraging because of the sad or bright attitude of the mind.

When the individual sinks below the level of circumstances, he surrenders himself to the influence of bad times, ill luck, and sorrow. If he rises above circumstances by the heroic courage that is in him, all conditions of life, however dark and threatening, will be like the blanket of mist that disappears with the warm glance of the sun. The sorrows of the normal man are not inherent in the conditions of life. They are born out of the weaknesses of the human mind. Awaken the victor in yourself, arouse the sleeping hero in yourself, and lo! No sorrow will ever darken your door.

CHAPTER *2*

CALMNESS: THE SOURCE OF POWER

Every individual has a soul and a body. Through delusion, he finds his soul identified with the body and thus all the conditions of the body. The body can be injured, changed, and destroyed; it is limited and short lasting. So the individual identified with the body thinks himself vulnerable.

But the soul cannot in any way be injured, changed, or destroyed. The soul, made in the image of the Spirit, is ever calm, eternal, ever undisturbed.

By worldly desires, an individual becomes more and more identified with the weakness of the body, always fearing death and limitations. If the soul directs its attention away from the misery-making bodily limitations, and meditates until his delusion vanishes, he finds himself as the everlasting soul, living in the fortress of omnipresence: impregnable, invulnerable to any effects of delusive vibratory change. Every individual must remember that he is immortal, not open to any invasion of change or death, even when his body appears to be affected by disease, accident, or death.

By concentrating on the soul, the individual can do away with mortal desires, and find everlasting freedom.

No matter how long you have been meditating, if you still fear bodily diseases or death, and have not realized the immortality of the soul, you have advanced little and have realized little. You must meditate more and more deeply until you have ecstatic communion with God and forget the limitations of the body. During meditation you must *realize* that you are far above all bodily changes—formless, omnipresent, omniscient.

&

Life is change.

Remain ever calm within. Be even-minded. When working, be calmly active. Someday, you will know yourself to be subject no longer to the tides of Destiny. Your strength will come from within; you will not depend on outer incentives of any kind for motivation.

As a devotee on the spiritual path, give little weight to the trials that beset you. Be even-minded. Walk with courage. Go forward from day to day with calm, inner faith. Eventually, you will pass beyond every shadow of bad karma, beyond all tests and difficulties, and will behold at last the dawn of divine fulfillment. In that highest of all states of consciousness will come freedom from every last, trailing vapor of misfortune.

Today—now!—set out for that promised land—distant-seeming, yet ever near: the unshakable state of absolute fulfillment in God.

O Devotee, make haste!

❦

Play your tragic or comic parts in life with an inner smile.

You are immortals, endowed with eternal joy. Never forget this during your play with changeable mortal life. This world is but a stage on which you play your parts under the direction of the Divine Stage Manager. Play them well, whether they be tragic or comic, always remembering that your real nature is eternal bliss, and nothing else. The one thing that will never leave you is the joy of your soul.

Therefore, learn to swim in the calm sea of unchanging bliss before you attempt to plunge into the maelstrom of material life, which is the realm of sorrow, pleasure, indifference, and a deceptive, temporary peace.

The whole-hearted practice of meditation brings deep bliss. Manifest this serenity always.

❦

How can you obtain poise? If it is difficult to earn money, it is much more difficult to obtain poise. Make a triangle, and on one side write "SWEETNESS," on the other side write "CALMNESS," and at the base write "HAPPINESS."

People have two kinds of natures: the private nature and the public nature. The private nature is when they relax and allow themselves to express ugliness. Many people dress up to go out, but inside passions are raging. Inside the house they say, "I am angry." Outside, "Oh, how *are* you?"

We must have unity of mind, speech, and body. Be calm in speech and in mind. Attain calmness; attain peace; attain happiness; attain poise.

Every night before going to bed, say: "I am the Prince of Peace sitting on the throne of Poise." Poise is your center. Whether you act quickly or slowly, you will never lose your kingly attitude of peace.

Many people know the way to peace and permanent happiness but are slow to follow it. They take lessons, then forget. Make use of your spiritual training. Live a godly life yourself, and everyone who crosses your path will be helped just by contact with you. If you want to live in peace and harmony, affirm divine calmness and peace, and send out only thoughts of love and goodwill.

"Be even-minded in the face of pleasure or pain, gain or loss, victory or defeat. In this way, you will incur no sin."
Bhagavad Gita, Chapter 2, Stanza 38

The above stanza can be interpreted to give guidance to the worldly man, the moral individual, and the spiritual aspirant:

Anyone who seeks business prosperity should keep his mind unruffled through sudden material gains or losses. A businessman who is not over-elated by success finds that his concentration is not deflected from the path of even greater success. On the other hand, the businessman who becomes depressed by business failure loses the focusing power of his concentration, and thus is unable to make renewed efforts for material success.

Every worldly man seeking success must keep his mind calm to meet the constantly changing circumstances of his life. He must be able, like a tractor, to move easily over ups and downs in the field of life.

The moral aspirant should not be overjoyed when he is victorious over a mighty temptation, nor should he be discouraged if he finds himself suddenly a prisoner of temptation. The resolute, even-minded moral individual moves steadily forward until he reaches his goal of complete self-mastery. Premature joy of temporary success or depression due to temporary failure should not be allowed to obstruct the way of moral progress.

Finally, when a spiritual devotee, after a few years of deep meditation, acquires a divine joy, he should not be over-confident in the lasting quality of that experience, until he reaches the final beatitude. Many devotees become self-satisfied with the superconscious joy of the soul and with beholding a few astral lights. They do not make further deep efforts at meditation, and thus fail to unite their consciousness with the omnipresent joy and light of Spirit.

A devotee who meditates regularly but finds himself the victim of a sudden explosion of subconscious restlessness should not be discouraged nor stop making renewed efforts at deeper meditation and God-contact. Until one is anchored in the Infinite, he must valiantly race his mental ship of concentration on the calm or rough seas of inner experiences until he reaches the shores of unending communion with the Infinite.

A yogi whose mind is like a rippleless lake, free from the waves of temporary mental elation, sadness, or emotional disturbances—due to loss or gain, victory or failure—finds within himself the unruffled clear reflection of the Spirit.

An unruffled calmness can be gained by deep and deeper meditation. This constant calmness ultimately becomes like an all-penetrating light which runs through all matter into the heart of the omnipresent Spirit. The aspiring yogi must keep his mind steadily fixed on the inner perception acquired by meditation, and should not allow his mind to be ruffled by the temporary outbursts of superconscious joy, or the temporary explosions of subconscious restlessness. Such a yogi finds his unchangeable altar of calmness the resting place of the ever-new, joyous Spirit.

Remember that He is always beside you, guiding and encouraging you. Learn to listen inwardly, all through the day, to this guiding Voice.

No matter what you are doing, if work seems exhausting, confusing, or impossible, just say within, "Father, this is your work. Willingly I give myself to serve You." Immediately all tension will be released, and the task will seem easy.

❧

Calmness is more dynamic and more powerful than peace. Calmness gives the devotee power to overcome all the obstacles in his life. Even in human affairs, the person who can remain calm under all circumstances is invincible.

❧

Affirmations for Calmness

The moment my mind is agitated, restless, or disturbed, I will retire to silence, discrimination, and concentration until calmness is restored.

The light of Christ shines through me, and therefore my mind is clear. Order and harmony reign in all my affairs.

Happiness, understanding, the joy of creative expression, and perfect peace and poise can be mine only when I concentrate all my power and ability upon expressing the Father's will.

⁂

Never let your mind be seduced by restlessness, through joking too much, too many distractions, and so on. Be deep. As soon as you succumb to restlessness, all the old troubles will begin to exert their pull on the mind once again: sex, wine, and money.

Of course, a little fun and laughter is good, occasionally. I, too, like to laugh sometimes, as you know. But when I choose to be serious, nothing and no one can draw me out of my inner Self.

Be deep in everything you do. Even when laughing, don't lose your inner calmness. Be joyful inside, but always inwardly a little withdrawn. Be centered in the joy within.

Dwell always in the Self. Come down a little bit when you have to, to eat, or talk, or to do your work; then withdraw into the Self again.

Be calmly active, and actively calm. That is the way of the yogi.

❧

Desire and anger are the two greatest barriers to wisdom. They destroy a person's peace of mind, and obstruct the flow of his understanding. When anger seizes you, you may think, "Oh, this feels wonderful!" In exhilaration, you may do something terrible, not even counting the cost.

Desire, again, confuses the mind. Frustrated desire is what produces anger. It is important that you always remain inwardly calm and non-attached. Accept with an unruffled mind whatever comes. I often say, "What comes of itself, let it come." This is just as true for the bad things in life as for the good. Only calmness will give you a sense of correct proportion. It will inspire you to behave with unfailing good sense.

❧

Some time ago a man suffering from a chronic nervous heart came to me for healing. He said, "I have tried many things, but I am unable to get rid of my heart trouble."

After calm, intuitive reflection, I told him to bring me a pair of scissors. Alarmed and suspicious, he stared at me, and remonstrated, "Sir, are you going to perform an incision on my heart?!" I laughed and replied, "I am not a doctor, and you have never heard of anyone using scissors for operating upon the heart."

When he reluctantly brought the scissors, I cut off one of his vest buttons and told him not to replace the button and not to touch the place where the missing button belonged. I asked him to come back after fifteen days, and told him I expected him to be healed by that time.

The man laughingly exclaimed, "I will do what you say since I believe in you, but of all the crazy cures, I think this is the craziest."

After fifteen days he came to me, shouting with joy, and said, "The specialists say I am healed of my nervous heart. Sir, what did you do? Did you dispossess the button of a ghost?"

With a smile I said, "Yes, I did! Your hand was constantly fiddling with the vest button near your heart. This button was the 'ghost' nagging your heart into a nervous fit. Your heart, freed from the disturbing vest button, has ceased to trouble you."

CHAPTER 3

CONFIDENCE: YOU ARE A CHILD OF THE INFINITE

The Creative Spiritual Consciousness abides within the soul of man, and he may do with it whatever he wishes, for he has been created in the image of God with unlimited powers. He is the master of his own destiny, if he will but accept and use that God-given power. The only limitation on man is imposed by himself, through his thoughts. It is a well-known psychological fact that "Thoughts are things." The statement in Proverbs, "As a man thinketh in his heart, so is he," is a truth which has revolutionized and transformed the lives of thousands.

❧

Cultivate the consciousness that the Divine Spirit is your own Father and is the owner of the whole universe, along with all of its abundance. You, as His beloved child, have the absolute right to possess anything, even as He does. Never beg or pray for anything, but hold the thought that you have everything already, and that all you have to do is to seize it with the infinite, natural confidence of a child of God.

Don't be a beggar! Realize that you are the child of the Emperor of the Universe.

❧

God answers all prayers. Restless prayers, however, He answers only a little bit. If you offer to others something that isn't yours to give, won't that be an empty gesture? Similarly, if you pray to God, but lack control over your own thoughts, that prayer will have no power. Thoughts and feelings, both, must be focused when you pray. Otherwise, God will meet your little trickle with another trickle of His own! He will dole out His answers to you in a teaspoon. Too often, prayer is more like the halfhearted mumbling of a beggar than the confident, loving demand of a friend.

❧

Just as a child lives happily and confidently secure in the protecting power of its parents, so also does the devotee, by becoming a divine child, relinquish all fear and depend completely on the all-protecting power of God.

By contrast, the person who does not cultivate the child-like qualities latent in the soul is constantly tortured by self: shyness, worries, fear, and attachments, which drown his peace in an ocean of misery.

Before our Heavenly Father we should be like little children. He likes that. He doesn't need from us carefully contrived theological definitions, or prayers that are chiseled to perfection lest they offend His imperial ears. He wants us to love Him in all simplicity, just like children.

⌘

If failures invade you repeatedly, don't get discouraged. They should act as stimulants, not poisons, to your material or spiritual growth. The period of failure is the best season for sowing the seeds of success.

Every new effort after a failure must be well planned and charged with increasing intensity of attention. If a bad habit bothers you, do two things: Negatively, try to avoid it and everything that occasioned or stimulated it, without concentrating on it in your zeal to avoid it. Positively, divert your mind to some good habit, and keep it furiously engaged in culturing it, until it becomes a part of yourself.

The more you improve yourself, the more you will elevate others around you.

⌘

Praise does not make you better, nor blame worse, than what you are. Then why heed these two? Don't pay attention when people praise you, but survey yourself carefully when they blame you. If you are at fault, free yourself from error quickly; but if you are not guilty, laugh and forget it. Truth will speak for you.

∞

Affirmations for Confidence

As a perfect pattern for an oak tree is encased in the acorn, so a perfect pattern for my life was placed in me in the beginning. I shall endeavor to let this perfect plan emerge into manifestation without hindrance.

I have within me the power and intelligence I need to meet all the problems of this day. I shall live today in perfect faith, calling on this power as the need arises.

I will not limit my thoughts. I am Life, Intelligence, Health, Joy, Peace, and Power. This is the essential truth of my Being, and I shall try to express these qualities completely.

I will transform all conditions, good or bad, into instruments of success. Before a conquering soul, even dangers loom as benedictions from God.

The sunshine of God's prosperity has just burst through the dark sky of my limitations. I am His child. What He has, I have.

I realize that God's power is limitless, and, since I am made in His image, I, too, have power to overcome all obstacles.

I know that each seeming difficulty is but a call to release the power which I already possess. As I express this power, I grow stronger and wiser.

Since God, or Good, is everywhere present at all times, my good is always with me, waiting for me to call it into manifestation. I shall go forth in perfect faith in the power of omnipresent Good to bring me what I need, when I need it.

Come out of your closed chamber of mental stagnation and narrowness. Drink in the fresh air of others' vital thoughts and views. Receive mental nourishment from materially and spiritually progressive minds. Feast unstintingly on creative thinking within yourself and others. Take long mental walks on the paths of self-confidence. Exhale poisonous thoughts of discouragement, discontentment, and hopelessness. Inhale the fresh oxygen of success, and know that you are progressing with God's help. This will recharge your soul battery. By consciously experiencing God's bliss through meditation, you can consciously destroy mental stagnation and acquire increasing spiritual health and wisdom.

Eliminate all mental poisons and partake of the divine nourishment of determination, courage, continuous mental effort, and concentration. You will learn to overcome the most difficult problems with ease.

There are many avenues through which outer influences percolate into the mind and form the inner environment. Don't let unhealthy materials float down the stream of your habit-forming thoughts. Watch the quality of the books you read. Watch the kind of people with whom you associate. Watch the influence upon you of family, country, and daily associates. Many people are unsuccessful because their families have infected their subconscious minds with progress-paralyzing, discouraging thoughts, such as: "Oh John, no matter what you try, you make a mess of it."

Disabuse yourself. Wake up! Remember, no one can affect your happiness unless you yourself choose to be unhappy. If you have made up your mind to keep your own inner happiness under all conditions, then no one can make you unhappy.

Affirm: Whatever conditions confront me, I know that they represent the next step in my unfoldment. I welcome all tests, no matter how trying, because I know that within me is the intelligence to understand, and the power to overcome. I am willing to learn the lesson each experience can teach, and I am thankful for the strength and understanding developed by overcoming each trial.

⚬

Written in 1934:

Now, when everybody is going about crying "Depression," is the time to depress depression. Even if you have no job, for your own good and for the good of everybody else, you should not be depressed. If you sit in your home moaning about the depression, you do an injustice to yourself by paralyzing your mind with sorrow, instead of keeping it busy with the creative thinking that can show you a way out of your difficulties.

I can forgive the physically lazy man if his body is weak or if it needs rest, but I cannot so easily forgive the inwardly fossilized man, who is too lazy to think. Such individuals fear to exercise their brains lest they succeed! It is an injustice to your own progressive powers to keep them crippled by sorrow. Instead of sobbing, you must keep your mind busy with continuous, energetic thinking as to how you can secure work for yourself. You must make the businesses in your city so uncomfortable with your never-silent advertisement of yourself, your creative genius, and your ability to work, that they will be glad to give you a job, if only to make you keep quiet. Then, when you are hired, you must show your employers that you are indispensable to them, and that you can do for them what no one else can.

Darkness flies away before the light. By continually crying "Abundance," you will chase away the thought of depression. If you are suffering materially, do not add more injury to yourself by mentally accepting defeat. You can kindle hope in the hearts of your family and your neighbors with the tapers of courage, will power, and creative thinking.

Remember that self-confidence and abundance-consciousness spread faster than the disease of depression ever can. Just as the sun quickly spreads over half the globe at one time, so the strength of your joy and abundance-consciousness can spread quickly over the dark territories of your own consciousness, as well as that of your family, your neighbors, your country, and the whole world.

❧

If you have an inferiority complex, remember that success, health, and wisdom are your rightful heritage. Your difficulty is due to weakness, which may have had its inception in one or more factors. It can be overcome by determination, courage, common sense, and faith in God and in yourself.

Therefore, if you are firmly convinced that you are a failure, change your mental attitude at once. Be unshakable in your conviction that you have all the potentialities of great success.

❧

No matter what your trials have been, or how discouraged you are, if you will make a continued effort to be better, you will find that, being made in the image of God, you are endowed with an unlimited power that is much stronger than your worst trials. Make up your mind that you will win, focusing all your concentration on ceaseless efforts to succeed, and you will surely be victorious.

Remember that your past difficulties did not come to crush you, but to strengthen your determination to use your limitless divine powers to succeed. God wants you to conquer the difficult tests of life and to come back to His home of wisdom.

CHAPTER *4*

RIDDING THE MIND OF WORRY, FEAR, AND NERVOUSNESS

Worries are often the result of attempting to do too many things too quickly. Do not "bolt" your mental duties, but thoroughly masticate them, one at a time, with the teeth of attention, and saturate them with the saliva of good judgment. Thus, will you avoid worry indigestion.

Do not feed your mind with mental poisons of worries. Learn to remove the causes of your worries without permitting them to worry you.

If you are suffering from mental "ill health," go on a mental fast. A health-giving mental fast will clear the mind and rid it of the accumulated mental poisons from a careless mental diet.

Go on worry fasts. Three times a day, shake off all worries. At seven o'clock in the morning, say to yourself, "All my worries of the night are cast out, and from 7 to 8 a.m. I refuse to worry, no matter how troublesome are the duties ahead of me. I am on a worry fast." From noon to 1 p.m., say, "I am cheerful, I will not worry." In the evening, between six and nine o'clock, while in the company of your spouse or hard-to-get-along-with relatives or friends, mentally make a strong resolution: "Within these three hours I will not worry. I refuse to get vexed, even if I am nagged. No matter how tempting it is to indulge in a worry feast, I will resist the temptation. I must not sabotage my peace-heart by shocks of worries. I cannot afford to worry—I am on a worry fast." After you succeed in carrying out worry fasts during certain hours of the day, try fasting for one or two weeks at a time. Then, try to prevent the accumulation of worry poisons in your system entirely.

Whenever you find yourself indulging in a worry feast, go on a partial or complete worry fast for a day or a week. Whenever you make up your mind not to worry, stick to your resolution. You can calmly solve your most difficult problems, putting forth your greatest effort, and at the same time absolutely refuse to worry. Tell your mind, "I am satisfied and happy that I am doing my best to solve my problem; there is absolutely no reason to worry."

When you are on a worry fast, drink copiously of the fresh waters of peace flowing from the spring of every circumstance, vitalized by your determination to be cheerful. If you have made up your mind to be cheerful, nothing can make you unhappy. If you choose not to destroy your peace of mind by worrying about unhappy circumstances, none can make you dejected.

Concern yourself only with the untiring performance of right actions, and not with their results. Leave the results to God, saying, "I have done my best under the circumstances; therefore, I am happy."

Worry fasting is the negative method for overcoming worry poisoning. There is also a positive method: One infected with the germs of worry must feast frugally, but regularly, on the society of joyful minds. Every day he must associate—if only for a little while—with "joy-infected" minds. There are some people the song of whose laughter nothing can still. Seek them out, and feast with them on this most vitalizing food of joy. Steadfastly continue your laughter diet, and at the end of a month or two you will see the change—your mind will be filled with sunshine.

The mind must manifest calmness. Where the worries and trials of everyday life are concerned, the mind must be like water, which does not retain any impression of the waves that play on its surface.

This is not an excuse for negligence in business, which should be avoided as carefully as the unnecessary concern arising from an inflated sense of responsibility. You must remember that without health, peace, and happiness, material success is of little value to you. What does it avail you if you become seriously ill from worry?

Therefore, let go of your worries. Enter into absolute silence every morning and night, and banish thoughts for several minutes each time. Then, visualize some happy incident in your life; mentally go through the pleasant experience over and over again until you forget your worries entirely.

Mental relaxation is the ability to free the attention at will from haunting worries over past and present difficulties, the pressure of constant responsibilities, dread of accidents, and disturbing thoughts and attachments. Mastery in mental relaxation comes with faithful practice. It can be attained by freeing the mind of all thoughts at will, and keeping the attention fixed on peace and contentment within.

☙

Fear is a mental poison, unless it is used as an antidote — a stimulus to spur a person on to calm caution. Fear draws to itself the objects of fear, as a magnet draws to itself pieces of iron.

Fear intensifies and magnifies our physical pain and mental agonies a hundredfold. Fear is destructive to the heart, nervous system, and brain. It is destructive to mental initiative, courage, judgment, common sense, and will power. Fear shrouds the soul's all-conquering confidence and power.

When something is threatening to harm you, do not throttle your creative mental powers with fear. Instead, use fear as a goad to find practical solutions to avoid danger.

When something is threatening you, do not sit idle—do something about it, calmly mustering all the power of your will and judgment.

Fear of failure or sickness is nourished by thinking constantly of dire possibilities, until these take root in the subconscious and finally in the superconscious. These fear seeds germinate and fill the mind with fear plants bearing poisonous, fear fruits.

If you are unable to dislodge the haunting fear of failure or ill health, divert your mind by turning your attention to interesting, absorbing books, or even to harmless amusements. After the mind forgets its haunting fear, encourage it to discover and root out the causes of failure and ill health in the soil of your daily life.

⁓

Do not fear disease or accidents if you have had them once. Rather, fear to be afraid, for such fear will create disease- and accident-consciousness, and if it is strong enough, you will draw to yourself the very things you most fear.

On the other hand, fearlessness will, in all probability, avert them, or at least minimize their power.

Kill fear by refusing to be afraid. Know that you are safe behind the battlements of God's eternal safety, even though you are rocked on seas of suffering, or find death knocking at your door. God's protecting rays can dispel the menacing clouds of doomsday, calm the waves of trials, and keep you safe, whether you are in a castle or on the battlefield of life, with bullets of trials flying around you.

❧

When fear comes, tense and relax, and exhale several times. Switch on the electricity of calmness and nonchalance. Let your whole mental machinery wake up and actively hum with the vibration of will. Then, harness the power of will to the cogwheels of fearless caution and good judgment. Continuously revolve these to produce practical ideas for escaping your specific, impending calamity.

❧

A mental indulgence in fear will create a subconscious fear habit. Then, when something upsetting to the regular routine occurs, the subconscious fear habit will assert itself, magnify the object of your fears, and paralyze the will-to-fight-fear faculty of the conscious mind. Man is made in the image of God and has all the powers and potentialities of God; therefore, it is wrong for him to think that trials are greater than his divinity. Remember, no matter how great your trials, you are able to conquer them. God will not allow you to be tempted and tried beyond your strength.

Fear should not produce mental inertia, paralysis, or despondency. Instead, it should spur you on to calm, cautious activity, avoiding equally rashness and timidity.

Uproot fear from within by forceful concentration on courage—and by shifting your consciousness to the absolute peace within. Associate with healthy and prosperous people who do not fear sickness or failure.

❧

Stage fright is a form of fear which causes nervousness in many people, so that they are unable to do anything naturally. If you are shy and have stage fright, get your mind quiet and remember that all the power you need is within you—all the power to convince people, all the power to let the Infinite Spirit function through you.

Stage fright and timidity should be supplanted by deep attention, concentration, and calmness just before appearing on the stage. Practice the following:

1. Deep breathing: Breathe deeply a few times, concentrating at the point between the eyebrows, just before the performance. This will remove timidity and insure self-confidence.

2. Mentally rehearse very clearly how masterfully, joyously, and eagerly you are going to perform.

3. Remove nervousness by tensing and relaxing.

4. Take a bath two hours before, or immediately before, the performance. If time is limited, simply wash all the openings of the body with cold water.

5. Humbleness is magnetic and will draw kind attention and sympathy from your audience, while pride will cause sneers and apathy. An inferiority complex will cause pity, disbelief, and lack of enthusiasm in your audience. An inferiority complex will cause you to underestimate your real ability and will destroy whatever faculty you may possess. Cool confidence in your ability and the positive outcome of your performance, due to God working with you, must always keep you happy and contented just before your debut. Make up your mind to do your very utmost to make people appreciate your performance.

6. Get the finest teacher to acquaint you with the best technique of acting, speaking, or singing, and then, with all your inspiration and attention, master the technique as your own.

7. Eat very sparingly, say at 2 p.m., for an 8 o'clock performance. A stomach loaded with food absorbs the power of the attention needed for the performance.

You must practice your technique with intelligence, inspiration, and God-intoxication every day. Try to feel, in whatever good work you do, that God is working through you.

⁓

One form of fear is the fear of death. Death should be regarded as a universal experience, a change that everyone passes through. It should be looked upon as good, as a new opportunity, as a rest from the weary struggle on this earth. Besides, there is nothing to fear, because as long as you are not dead, you are alive; when you are dead, it is all over and there is nothing to worry about.

Fear of death is born of the greatest ignorance, and it paralyzes activity, thought, and ambition. Live today well, and the next step will take care of itself. Console yourself with the thought that death happens to everybody—saint or sinner—and that therefore it must be a holiday from the troublesome business of life.

◈

Nervousness appears to be a simple ailment, but in reality it is very complicated and very uncomfortable. If you are nervous, it is difficult to heal any disease you might have. If you are nervous, you cannot concentrate and work efficiently to attain success. If you are nervous, you cannot meditate deeply and thus acquire peace and wisdom. In fact, nervousness interferes with all the normal functioning of the human body and mind. It upsets the physical, mental, and spiritual machinery.

Nervousness may be caused by great and continuous excitement, such as excessive stimulation of the senses, thoughts, or emotions. Lack of the necessities for normal and happy living—such as proper exercise, fresh air, sunshine, right food, agreeable work, and a purpose in life—aggravate, if they do not actually cause, a condition of nervousness. Nervousness is highly contagious and may also be caused by association with nervous, faultfinding, or otherwise disagreeable people.

Any continued mental or physical excitement disturbs the balance of the flow of life force through the nerves. If you put a two-thousand-volt current through a fifty-watt light bulb, it will destroy the bulb. In the same way, too great a stimulation upsets the functioning of the nervous system. When electric wires in a factory are destroyed, they can be replaced by an electrician, but when your nerves are damaged you can do nothing to replace them.

Analyze yourself and discover that anger, fear, worry, and all such emotions cause nervousness. Fear and worry are closely connected: worry is usually fear that something undesirable is going to happen. What you fear rarely happens—a calm analysis of the situation will often remove the worry.

When you are angry, your brain cells burn. When you worry, you paralyze the nerves. Fear burns the nerves that bring energy to the heart. Feeling timid destroys the nerve endings. Too much sleep drugs the nerves, and too little sleep is hurtful to nerves. The cure is to be calm at all times and to do your best. When you are worried about something, you must first find out the facts, do your best, and laugh at the world. You will find that God's law will protect you.

Remember, God is with you. The more you meditate and try to contact Him, the more often you will feel Him with you. Fear is an unnecessary emotion. You must not be afraid of anything.

$$\mathbb{\alpha}$$

For ordinary nervousness, take a cold shower or splash your face with cold water. Partial fasting—to go without breakfast or lunch—is helpful. Have a good diet, but above all, keep the company of cool, calm people.

Always be calm; be calmly active and actively calm. Get away from the city once in a while.

Most importantly, learn the method of controlling energy. Your body is like a little bubble of energy in the cosmic sea of energy. You can contact cosmic energy and bring that energy into your body through the Energization Exercises.[*]

$$\mathbb{\alpha}$$

To be nervous is to be in Hades. To be calm is to be with God. Eat right, fast once a week, keep your spine straight,

[*]   Yogananda developed a series of exercises, called the *Energization Exercises*, for consciously recharging the body with energy. A booklet of these exercises is available, published by Crystal Clarity Publishers: 800-424-1055.

learn the methods of meditation and energization, be free from poisons, and attain perfect freedom from all nervousness.

❧

Definition: Nervousness is a restless mind vibrating through the nerves.

Psychological symptoms of nervousness:

- Impatience
- Want of discretion in action
- Being influenced by the contagious temperament of others
- Fear, anger, jealousy
- Highstrung imagination
- Ceaseless brain-storm (too much jazz, theatre-going, dancing)
- Purposeless life, exciting existence
- Mind and reason enslaved by nerves
- Exciting dreams

Psycho-physical symptoms of nervousness:

Shaking of head or hand, twitching lips, restless fingers, involuntary movement of body parts, fits, heart trouble, stimulated vision (hallucinations), hasty action (nerves act before the mind intends), garrulous or chatterbox habits, insomnia.

Physical aids for curing nervousness:

- Avoid sour pickles, spices, onions, and stimulants.
- Enjoy celery, orange, or almond juice, and almond butter.
- Treat indigestion and avoid constipation.
- Reduce hasty actions and nervous habits, such as scratching, playing with fingers, wrinkling the face.
- Reduce over-working.
- Take frequent baths, rubbing the hands on the skin of the entire body before bath.
- Go to bed early.
- Don't lie awake in bed in the morning—wake up and get up.

- Practice sexual moderation.
- Tense the body and inhale; exhale, and release tension and nervousness with the exhalation.
- Take brisk fresh-air walks daily.

Psychological and general means of cure:

- Avoid argumentation and quarrelsome surroundings.
- Delay action a little after resolution.
- Don't remain in the same room with nervous people.
- Choke excitement in the bud.
- Avoid jazz and loud music for some time at least.
- Listen to violin music.
- Don't frequent movies which contain exciting scenes or tragedies.
- Sleep alone, and empty your body and mind of thoughts and sensations before you sleep.
- Fully analyze what you fear or what you are excited about. Refuse to accept sudden emotions and excitement. Find the cause of excitement and seek a remedy;

do not allow anxiety to rule the mind. Refuse to be obsessed by one idea.

• Keep company with people superior to you in everything—people of cool and sweet temperament.

• Don't indulge in vulgar jokes.

• Practice calmness, and do not talk too much.

• Practice concentration and meditation, and hold on to their calm after-effects.

Most cases of nervousness are psychological, expressing through the body, and simple analysis from a doctor or psychoanalyst, or through personal introspection, can effect an immediate cure.

Above all, *moderation* in eating, bodily enjoyments, sex impulses, work, money making, and social functions leads to happiness, health, and mental efficiency.

The best way to get rid of nervousness is first to keep the right company. Tell me what kind of company a person keeps, and I will tell you what he is. We always love the company of those who flatter us, but flattery weakens us. We should like the company of those who tell us the truth and help us to be better. If we live always in the company of flatterers, it is bad for our spiritual growth.

Once there was a man who criticized everything a certain master did. That man died, and the disciples joyously told their guru, "Master, the man who was always criticizing you is dead." The Master began to weep. The disciples were surprised and said, "Why do you weep? You should be glad to be rid of this terrible man!" The Master replied, "No, I am sorry, my teacher is dead." He found the man's criticism helpful. To criticize is bad, but if you can stand criticism, it is wonderful.

Be careful in your choice of company. Keep company with people who are calm, strong, and wise, with a deeper nature than you have. When a criminal is put into the company of a greater criminal, it does not help him. When it is time for him to leave prison, the warden says, "When are you coming back?" When nervous people are in the company of other nervous people, they cannot get better.

Association with strong, happy, serene, kind, and spiritual people is of great benefit to the nervous person. Even a few moments' company with a saint can work wonders in producing calmness and quiet. A real holy man acts as a raft to carry you away from suffering.

❧

There is a common form of nervousness: soul nervousness. The soul is so identified with the body that it has forgotten its real nature. Soul nervousness can be destroyed only by meditation—by transferring the attention from your nerves to the perception of Infinite Happiness within, transferring your attention from the bundle of bodily sensations to the infinite nature which is your true Self.

When you have health, you want wealth, and when you have both, you want happiness. Nothing will satisfy you until you find God. Your nervousness will disappear when you realize that you are one with God. Your spiritual Self is calling you every day. You must realize that you are not this body, but the Infinite Spirit within.

❧

Chapter 5

Uprooting Other Negative Emotions

Remind yourself always:

I have the most fascinating task to perform. It keeps me so occupied that there is no time or energy left to worry about the affairs of other people. I am engaged in the business of lifting myself from ignorance to understanding and enlightenment. It requires all of my attention to rid my thoughts and emotions of anger, jealousy, pride, revenge, fear, sense of lack, and sickness. These hindrances I must catch and cast out forever, so that when the debris of negation is cleared away, the pure water of life itself may spring forth and flow freely through me to bless all. This is my work. How can I be concerned with anything less?

Anger is not an antidote for anger. A strong wrath may bring suppression of a weaker wrath, but it will never kill it. When you are angry, say nothing. Think of anger as a disease, like a cold, and break it up by mental warm baths of thinking of those with whom you could never be angry, no matter how they behave. If your anger is too violent, take a cold shower, douse the head with cold water, or put ice on the medulla and the temples just above the ears, on top of the head, and on the forehead, especially between the eyebrows.

When anger comes, start your machinery of calmness going; let your calmness move the cogwheel of peace, love, and forgiveness. With these antidotes, destroy anger. As you do not want others to be angry with you, so you do not wish others to feel your ugly anger. Think of love. When you become Christlike and look upon all humanity as little brothers hurting one another (for they know not what they do), then you cannot feel angry with anyone. Ignorance is the mother of all anger.

Develop metaphysical reason and destroy anger. Look upon your anger-arousing agent as a child of God, a little five-year-old baby brother who unknowingly perhaps stabbed you. You must not feel a desire to stab this little brother in return. Mentally destroy anger by saying: "I will not poison my peace by anger; I will not disturb my habitual joy-giving calmness by wrath."

◈

When a desire of yours is obstructed, it usually results in anger. First, find out whether your desire was good or bad. If it was bad, you should be grateful to be released from wrongdoing. Be calm; be firm.

When wrath comes, you forget your position; when you forget your position you do wrong things, thereby becoming a tool of ignorance. If something has gone wrong, correct the error. Look at things intelligently and peacefully. The divine law will give you the right understanding.

If you want to conquer any person, make him break his sword. Conquer evil with love: That is divine strength. It is much stronger than anger. The person who is angry with you should draw from you an ocean of love and of calmness, which will quench the fire of his wrath. Learn to give love, calmness, and continuous understanding to those who are angry.

When you are angry, you are in a slow baking oven. All your nerves, brain cells, and flesh are baking in the fire of anger, which at times has caused even death. Anger carried to extremes is not safe for the body, mind, or soul. Many illnesses are caused by anger, which also distorts the face and brings on old age quickly. Do not in this way desecrate your face and mind, which are made in the image of God.

Jesus showed how great he was when he said, "Father, forgive them, for they know not what they do." He showed that he was God. If he had, in anger, used all the powers at his command to destroy others, would mankind worship Him today? No! He showed his Godlike qualities and is now enshrined in every heart. He is the luminary that we behold throughout eternity: a light to warm us and to give us strength.

❧

Each morning is the beginning of a new day and of a new year. As I cleanse my body and make it fit for the activity of the day, so shall I cleanse my mind of fear, prejudice, and all negation.

❧

When you are sick, do not concentrate upon the length of your suffering, but picture to yourself the fountain of youthful, healthful years that you have already enjoyed. What you have had, you can have again if you try hard enough. To give up is the difficult, miserable way in the long run, and to try hard until you succeed is the easiest way.

Banish sadness with joy; destroy sickening thoughts of failure with the tonic of success consciousness. Cast sorrows into the flames of happiness. Banish restlessness and ignorance from the shores of your mind. Establish the Kingdom of Silence within, and the God of Happiness will enter without prayer, invitation, or coaxing.

◌

An inferiority complex is born of contact with weak-minded people and the weak innate subconscious mind. A superiority complex comes from false pride and an inflated ego. Both inferiority and superiority complexes are destructive to self-development. Both are fostered by imagination, while neither belongs to the true, all-powerful nature of the soul. Develop self-confidence by conquering your weaknesses. Found your self-confidence on actual achievements, and you will be free from all inferiority and superiority complexes.

◌

Be silent and calm every night for at least ten minutes, preferably much longer, before you retire, and again in the morning before starting the day. This will produce an unbreakable inner habit of happiness, which will make you able to meet all the trying situations of the everyday battle of life. With that unchangeable happiness within, seek to fulfill your daily needs. Seek happiness more and more in your mind, and less and less in the desire to acquire things. Be so happy in your mind that nothing that comes can possibly make you unhappy.

Be happy because you know that you have acquired the power not to be negative, and because you know that you can acquire at will whatever you need.

 with unceasing blessing
Paramhansa Yogananda
1953

CHAPTER 6

SCIENTIFIC HEALING AFFIRMATIONS FOR INNER STRENGTH

Excerpted from *Scientific Healing Affirmations* by Paramhansa Yogananda, 1924 edition

THE SPIRITUAL POWER OF MAN'S WORD

Man's word is Spirit in man. Words are sounds occasioned by the vibrations of thoughts. Thoughts are vibrations sent forth by the ego or soul. Every word that leaves your mouth ought to be potent with genuine soul vibration. The words of most people are lifeless because they are spoken automatically, without being impregnated with soul force. Too much talking, exaggeration, or falsehood weakens the power of your words. That is why the prayers or words of such people do not produce any desired changes. Every word you speak must represent not only Truth, but also some of your own realized soul force. Words without soul force are like husks without the corn.

Words that are saturated with sincerity, conviction, faith, and intuition are like vibration bombs, which can explode the rocks of difficulties and create the change desired. Avoid speaking unpleasant words, even if they are true.

Sincere words or affirmations repeated understandingly, feelingly, and willingly are sure to move the omnipresent Cosmic Vibratory Force to render aid in your difficulty.

Appeal to that Force with infinite confidence, casting out all doubt. If your affirmations are spoken with disbelief, or while looking for the desired result, your attention is deflected from its goal. You should not sow the vibratory prayer seed in the soil of Cosmic Consciousness, and then continually dig it up to see if the desired result has germinated.

THE GOD-GIVEN POWER OF MAN

It should be remembered that there is nothing greater in power than Cosmic Consciousness or God. Thus, you should seek Its aid alone. This does not mean that you should make yourself passive, inert, or credulous, or that you should minimize the power of your mind. Remember, God helps those who help themselves. He gave you will power, concentration, faith, reason, and common sense to use to help heal yourself. But in using your will power or common sense, you must not rely solely on your ego and thus disconnect yourself from the Divine Force. Always feel that you are using your own *but God-given* power to heal yourself or others. A balance must be struck between the old idea of depending wholly on God, and the modern idea of depending wholly on the ego.

MENTAL RESPONSIBILITY FOR CHRONIC DISEASES

In trying to get rid of a physical difficulty by physical or mental methods, one often concentrates more on the gripping power of the disease than on the possibility of cure, and thus the disease becomes a mental as well as a physical habit. This is especially true in cases of nervousness, where the disease is felt long after it is physically cured. Each bodily sensation of disease or health cuts grooves on the brain-cells, which further awaken certain habits of disease or health.

The subconscious habit of disease- or health-consciousness exerts a strong influence on the continuity of chronic problems. Chronic mental or physical diseases always have a deep root in the subconscious mind. In a mental or physical disturbance, one ought to be able to pull out the roots from the subconscious mind. That is why all affirmations practiced by the conscious mind ought to be impressive enough to stay as mental habits in the subconscious mind, which in turn automatically influences the conscious mind. Strong conscious affirmation is thus reinforced through the medium of the subconscious.

Still stronger conscious will or devotion affirmations not only reach the subconscious but the superconscious, the magic storehouse of all miraculous mental powers.

Individual affirmations should be practiced willingly, feelingly, intelligently, and devotionally, once in a while loudly (when nobody is listening), but mostly mentally, silently, with ever-increasing intensity of attention. The attention from the very beginning of affirmation should steadily increase, and never be allowed to flag. Flagging attention should be repeatedly focused on its given task.

Attentive, intelligent repetition and patience are the creators of habits, and ought to be employed during all affirmations. Deep and long-continued affirmations for curing chronic afflictions should be practiced mentally until they become part of one's intuitional convictions. Unchanged or contrary results (if any) should be ignored. It is better to die (if death has to come) with the conviction of being cured than with the consciousness that a mental or bodily ailment is incurable.

Another fact should always be remembered: though death is the necessary end of the body according to present human knowledge, the time of death can be changed by the superconscious power of the soul. In order to reach the superconscious, affirmations must be free from all uncertainties, doubts, and inattention. Attention and devotion are lights that can lead even blindly uttered affirmations to the subconscious and the superconscious. The greater the power of attention and devotion, the farther they can usher the vibrations of different affirmations to their subconscious or superconscious destinations.

Cures According to Temperament

Imagination, convincing reason, faith, feeling, will, or action can be employed according to the nature of the individual. Few people understand this. Coué* wanted to cure all persons by auto-suggestion. But the intellectual man is not susceptible to suggestion; he needs to understand the power of the mind over the body. Auto-suggestion is also powerless to act on the man of strong will power. He needs stimulation of his will power instead of his imagination, if he wants to be cured of his ailment.

Yogoda† teaches, by the art of concentration and meditation, and control of will, how to use the life current directly for healing one's self and others. No one should ever

---

* Émile Coué (1857–1926) was a French pharmacist who taught a method of psychotherapy that involved frequent repetitions of the formula, "Every day in every way, I am becoming better and better."

† Yogoda is a name Yogananda created for describing his teachings. He translated it poetically as "harmonious development of all human faculties." Translated literally, it means, "that which imparts yoga, or divine union."

minimize the importance of repeated, ever-deeper efforts of will or imagination affirmations as given here to effect the cure of bad habits, or physical or mental troubles.

FAITH IS MORE IMPORTANT THAN TIME

Instantaneous healing of physical, mental, and spiritual diseases can occur at any moment. The accumulated darkness of ages is dispelled at once by bringing in the light, not by trying to chase out the darkness. One never can tell when he is going to be healed, so do not expect a cure at once, or at some distant day. Faith, not time, will determine when the cure will be effected. Results depend on the right awakening of life energy, and the mental and subconscious state of the individual.

Effort and attention are absolutely necessary to arouse faith or will or imagination. When stimulated, these automatically impel the Life Energy to effect a cure. Desire or expectation for results weakens the force of attention. Without will or faith, Life Energy remains asleep, and cure cannot take place.

It takes time to reawaken weakened will, faith, or imagination in a patient suffering from a chronic problem, because his brain cells are grooved with the consciousness of that problem.

CLASSIFICATION OF HEALING

1. Healing of bodily diseases.

2. Healing of psychological diseases, such as fear, anger, bad habits, failure consciousness, lack of confidence.

3. Healing of spiritual diseases, such as indifference, purposeless life, intellectual pride, dogmatism, skepticism, ignorance of one's own divinity.

It is of paramount importance that equal emphasis be given to the prevention and cure of all three kinds of disease. Each causes suffering and must, therefore, be remedied by every suitable method of cure.

Most people's attention is fixed solely on the cure of bodily diseases, because these are so tangible. People do not realize that their mental troubles of fear, despair, worry, anger, or lack of self-control, and their spiritual suffering through ignorance of the meaning of human life, are even more important and overpowering. All physical diseases originate in mental and spiritual inharmony. Ignorance of the laws of mental hygiene and of the spiritual art of living is responsible for all human bodily and material suffering. If the mind is free from the mental bacteria of anger, worry, fear, etc., and the soul is free from ignorance, no material disease or lack can follow.

To Prevent Mental Disease

Cultivate peace and faith in the Cosmic Consciousness. Free the mind from all disturbing thoughts, and fill it with poise and joy. Realize the superiority of mental healing over physical healing. Abstain from acquiring bad habits, which make life miserable.

To Prevent Spiritual Disease

Firmly believe that you are created in the image of the Father, and are therefore immortal and perfect even as He is. If a particle of matter is indestructible, as science has proved, then the soul is indestructible also. Matter undergoes change; the soul undergoes changing experiences. The death or change of the form of a thing does not destroy or change its essence.

Apply the experiences of peace and poise received during concentration and meditation to your daily life. Maintain your equilibrium amidst trying circumstances, and stand unshaken by others' violent emotions or by adverse events.

Body and Consciousness Created by Man in the Dream State

While dreaming, a man may find himself walking joyously in a beautiful garden when he suddenly sees the dead body of a friend. He becomes stricken with grief, sheds tears, suffers from headache, and feels his heart throb. He wakes up and laughs at his illusory dream experience. What is the difference between the experiences of the man while dreaming, and the experiences of his waking state? The awareness of matter and consciousness is present in both cases. The sleeping man creates matter and consciousness in his dream.

World Illusion

If such a delusive creation is possible to the dreaming man, it is not difficult to imagine that the infinitely powerful Cosmic Consciousness could create a more realistic and permanent dream in the human consciousness, by the power of *maya* (or delusion).

Those who seek health or happiness, or who dread disease or bereavement, are working under the false conviction that health is different from disease, that bereavement is different from joy. When man realizes his true nature, the dualities disappear and all lack is seen to be illusory, all desire vanishes.

For those who have not attained Cosmic Consciousness, it is not appropriate to deny the limited healing power of herbs and medicines. In using affirmations, there is no need to scorn physical methods of cure, for they are the outcome of investigation into God's material laws.

How to Practice Affirmations

Affirmations must be practiced with a loud intonation, fading into a whisper, and then into mental chanting only. With attention and devotion, and deep conviction, take the thought from the auditory sense of the conscious mind, to the subconscious mind, and then to the superconscious mind. These affirmations can cure those who believe in them.

Repetition of affirmations goes from: Loud chanting to whisper chanting to mental chanting to subconscious chanting, and, finally, to superconscious chanting.

Subconscious chanting becomes automatic, with internal consciousness only. Superconscious chanting happens when the deep internal chanting vibrations are converted into re-alization, and are established in the conscious, subconscious, and superconscious minds. Holding the attention unbrokenly on the real Cosmic Vibration, not on any imaginary sound, is superconscious chanting.

Superconsciousness, Not Unconsciousness

One very important point to bear in mind is that when passing from one state of chanting to another, the attitude of the mind should likewise change, and become deeper and more concentrated. The aim is to unite the chanter, chant, and the process of chanting into one. The mind must sink into the deepest conscious state—NOT unconsciousness or absent-mindedness—but such a focused concentrated state of absolute consciousness that all thoughts are sunk and merged into the one state, like particles drawn to an irresistible magnet.

Physiological Centers

During the different affirmations, notice should be taken of the physiological centers where the attention should be directed: for example, the heart center when feeling is concerned, the medulla as the source of energy, and the point between the eyebrows to awaken will. We want to cultivate a conscious power over the direction of attention to the centers of thought, feeling, and will. Individuals should dwell deeply on the inner meaning of the affirmation.

The attitude of one's mind should vary according to the affirmation: will affirmations should be accompanied by strong will; feeling affirmations by devotion; reason affirmations by intelligence and devotion; imagination affirmations by fancy and faith. In healing others, select an affirmation that is suitable to the active, imaginative, emotional, or thoughtful temperament of your patient.

In all affirmations intensity of attention is foremost, but continuity and repetition are very important. Impregnate your affirmations with your devotion, will, and faith—intensely and repeatedly—unmindful of the results.

Absolute faith in God and his true devotees is the greatest method of instantaneous healing. It is better to die in the attempt to arouse that faith than to die with an absolute reliance on medicine or matter.

DIRECTIONS FOR INDIVIDUAL AND GROUP PRACTICE

Time: *For the individual*—Immediately after awakening from sleep in the morning, or during the period of somnolence preceding sleep at night.

For the group—Any suitable time.

Place: Noiseless or quiet surroundings as far as possible. If the affirmations have to be practiced in a noisy place, just ignore the disturbance and devotedly attend to your exercise.

Method: Before starting to affirm, free the mind of all worries and restlessness. Choose your affirmation and repeat it first loudly, then softer and more slowly, until your voice becomes a whisper. Then gradually affirm it mentally only, without moving even the tongue or lips. Affirm mentally until you feel that you have merged into deep, unbroken concentration—conscious continuity of uninterrupted thought.

Then, if you continue with your mental affirmation and go deeper still, you will feel a great sense of increasing joy and peace come over you. During deep concentration, your affirmation will merge into the subconscious stream, only to come back later reinforced with power to influence your conscious mind through the law of habit. During the time of experiencing ever-increasing peace, your affirmation goes deeper into the superconscious reservoir, to return later laden with unlimited power, not only to influence your conscious mind, but also to materially fulfill your desires. Doubt not, and you shall witness the miracle of this scientific faith.

During group affirmations for curing physical or mental disease in self or others, care should be taken to affirm with an even tone, even mental force, even concentration, and even sense of faith and peace. Weaker minds lessen the united force born of such affirmations and can even sidetrack this flood of force from its superconscious destination. Do not make any bodily movements, become mentally restless, or disturb your neighbor. Bodily stillness alone is not enough; your concentration or restlessness will materially affect the desired result favorably or unfavorably.

The affirmation-seeds below are impregnated with the soul's inspiration. They should be watered by your faith and concentration, and sown in the soil of superconscious peace.

There are many processes involved between the sowing of the affirmation-seed and its fruition. All the conditions for its growth must be fulfilled in order to produce the desired result. The affirmation-seed must be a living one, free from the cankers of doubt, restlessness, or inattention; it should be sown in the minds and hearts of people with faith, concentration, devotion, and peace; it should be watered with deep, fresh repetitions.

Avoid mechanical repetition. This is the meaning of the Biblical commandment, "Do not take the name of the Lord thy God in vain." Repeat affirmations firmly and with intensity and sincerity, until such power is gained that one command from you would be enough to change your body cells, or to move your soul to the performance of miracles.

SUGGESTIONS FOR PRACTICE

1. Sit facing north or east.

2. Close your eyes, and concentrate your attention on the medulla, unless otherwise directed. Keep the spine erect, chest high, abdomen in. Relax completely. Take deep breaths and exhale thrice.

3. Relax the body and keep it motionless. Empty the mind of all restless thoughts, and withdraw it from all bodily sensations.

4. Fill your mind with devotion and with will, feeling the former in the heart and the latter in the point between the eyebrows. Cast away anxiety, distrust, and worry. Realize calmly that the divine law works and is all-powerful only when you do not shut it out by doubt or disbelief. Faith and concentration allow it to operate unhampered. Hold the thought that all bodily and mental states are changeable and curable, and that the idea of anything being chronic is a delusion.

5. Forget what it is that you want to be healed.

6. In group affirmations the leader should read the affirmations rhythmically, while standing. The audience should repeat after him with the same rhythm and intonation.

FOR HEALING OF UN-SUCCESS CONSCIOUSNESS

Success comes by obeying divine and material laws. Both spiritual and material success must be attained. Material success consists in acquiring all the necessities of life. Money making should be utilized to improve society, one's country, and the world. Make all the money you can by improving your community, country, or the world, but never do so by acting against others' interests.

There are mental, subconscious, and superconscious laws for success and for fighting failure.

If you want Divine Law or superconscious power to help you, you should not stop your conscious efforts, nor should you rely wholly on your own natural abilities. Consciously try to succeed and to fight failure, feeling at the same time that the Divine Law is helping your efforts to be successful. This method establishes a conscious connection with the Divine. Think that, as a child of God, you have access to all things that belong to your Father. Doubt not; when you want anything, cast away the consciousness of failure, and realize that all things are your own. Subconscious habits of ignorance and disbelief in this law have deprived us of our divine heritage. Those who crave to use the resources of Divine Supply must destroy this wrong mentality by steady effort, saturated with infinite confidence.

When the conscious, subconscious, and superconscious methods of success are combined, success will surely come. Try again, no matter how many times you have tried unsuccessfully.

Material Success Affirmation

Thou art my Father,
Success and joy.
I am Thy child,
Success and joy.
All the wealth of this earth,
All the riches of the universe,
Belong to Thee, belong to Thee.
I am Thy child.
The wealth of earth and universe
Belongs to me, belongs to me,
O belongs to me, belongs to me.
I lived in thoughts of poverty
And wrongly fancied I was poor,
So I was poor.

Now I am home, and Thy consciousness
Has made me wealthy, made me rich.
I am success, I am rich.
Thou art my Treasure, I am rich, I am rich.
Thou art everything, Thou art everything,
Thou art mine,
I have everything, I have everything.
I am wealthy, I am rich,
I have everything, I have everything.
I possess all and everything
Even as Thou dost, even as Thou dost.
I possess everything, I possess everything.
Thou art my wealth,
I have everything.

Spiritual success consists in consciously contacting Cosmic Consciousness, and in maintaining your peace and poise no matter what irremediable events of life, like the death of friends, come to you. When you lose a loved one by the law of Nature, you should not sorrow but rather should thank God that He gave you the great privilege of befriending one of His dear ones. Spiritual success comes by looking upon all things cheerfully and courageously, with the realization that everything is marching towards the highest goal.

Psychological Success Affirmation

I am brave, I am strong.
Perfume of success thoughts
Blows in me, blows in me.
I am cool, I am calm.
I am sweet, I am kind.
I am love and sympathy.
I am charming and magnetic,
I am pleased with all.
I wipe away the tears and fears,
I have no enemy,
Though some think they are so,
I am the friend of all.
I have no habits,
In eating, dressing, behaving.
I am free, I am free.
I command Thee, O Attention,
To come and practice concentration
On things I do, on works I do.
I can do everything
When so I think, when so I think.
In church or temple, in prayer mood,
My vagrant thoughts against me stood
And held my mind from reaching Thee,
And held my mind from reaching Thee.

Teach me to own again, O own again,
My matter-sold mind and brain
That I may give them to Thee,
In prayer and ecstasy,
In meditation and reverie.
I shall worship Thee
In meditation,
In the mountain breast, and seclusion.
I shall feel Thy energy
Flowing through my hands in activity.
Lest I lose Thee,
I shall find Thee in activity.

MORE AFFIRMATIONS[*]

With closed eyes, concentrate your attention at the point between the eyebrows, and repeat the following thrice:

I will, with my own will,
Which flows from Divine Will,
To be healthy, to be well,
To be prosperous and spiritual,
To be well, to be well.

[*]   Specific affirmations for courage, calmness, and confidence are found in Chapters 1, 2, and 3.

Close your eyes, concentrate on the heart throb, and repeat with devotion and feeling:

> Thou art love, Thou art love,
> I am Thine, Thou art mine,
> I am Thine, Thou art mine,
> I am love, I am love.
> Love is healthy, love is perfect,
> I am healthy, I am love,
> I am whole, I am perfect.

Concentrate on the navel center and imagine a luminous light there. Close your eyes. Feel the navel and repeat with imagination and devotion:

> Thou art Life, Thou art strength,
> Thou art mind, and imagination,
> Thou art thought, Thou art fancy,
> I am thought, I am fancy.
> In every way, in every way,
> I am like Thee, I am like Thee,
> I am whole, I am like Thee.

Concentrate on the medulla, close your eyes, and feeling or visualizing the light there, repeat:

> Thy cosmic current flows in me, flows in me,
> Through my medulla, flows in me, flows in me.
> I think and will the current to flow,
> In all my body the current to flow,
> In all my body the current to flow.
> I am charged, I am cured,
> I am charged, I am cured.
> Lightning flash goes through me.
> I am cured, I am cured.

Superconscious Method of Healing

Rise above breath, tune yourself to the Cosmic Vibration, and with increasing intensity of will and highest devotion, concentrating at the point between the eyebrows, float the following prayers or convictions to the Cosmic Vibration. Mentally appeal to the Cosmic Vibration, just as you would to your own father.

> O Holy Vibration,
> Thou art I, Thou art I,
> My soul is Thine, Thy spirit is mine.
> Thou art perfect, Thou hast all,
> I am Thy Child, I have all,

I have all, I have all.
My bouquet of sweetest devotion,
My love and highest adoration,
I lay in Thee, I lay in Thee.
What is mine, that is Thine,
What is Thine, that is mine.
I pray, with love, I pray
Be Thou mine, be Thou mine.
Thou art I, Thou art I,
Thou art bliss, I am bliss,
Thou art peace, I am peace.
Thou art whole, I am whole,
Thou art perfect, Perfection is mine.
Thou art bliss, I am bliss,
I am bliss, I am bliss.

Place your absolute faith in God and always believe His power is working in you, just behind your thoughts, prayers, and convictions, to give infinite strength to heal yourself and others.

Acknowledge Him working with you in everything, and you will have Him always with you.

In affirming "I am healthy," or "I am wise," the positive affirmation must be so strong that it completely crowds out any subconscious, discouraging, negative enemy thoughts, which may be whispering to you: "You fool, you will never succeed. You are a failure; wisdom is impossible for you." You must know that whatever you wish strongly, you can materialize in short order.

Disregard the time element while affirming. In practicing affirmations, the spiritual aspirant must be unfailingly patient. Believe you are inherently healthy when you want good health; believe you are inherently prosperous when you want prosperity; believe you are inherently wise when you want wisdom—then health, prosperity, and wisdom will manifest themselves in you.

Change the trend of your thought. Cast out all negative mental habits, substituting in their place wholesome, courageous thought habits, and applying these in daily life, with unshakable confidence.

Remember that an intelligent, purposeful individual can easily substitute a good mental habit for a bad one in a trice, by the mere wish. Therefore, if you have a physical, mental, or spiritual habit that impedes your progress, rid yourself of it now. Do not put it off.

◈

Chapter 7

Meditation to Attune to the Highest within You

Teach me not to drug myself with the opiate of restlessness. Each day I will meditate more deeply than yesterday. Each tomorrow I will meditate more deeply than today.

Today, with the soft touch of intuition, I will tune my soul radio and rid my mind of static restlessness, that I may hear Thy voice of cosmic vibration, the music of atoms, and the melody of love vibrating in my superconsciousness.

I will find perpetual celestial happiness within. Peace will reign in silence, or in the midst of activities. Let me hear Thy voice, O God, in the cave of meditation.

⟨⟩

Teach me, O Spirit, by meditation to stop the storm of breath, mental restlessness, and sensory disturbances raging in the lake of my mind. Let the magic wand of my intuition stop the gale of passions and unnecessary desires. On the rippleless lake of my mind, let me behold the undistorted reflection of the moon of my soul, glistening with the light of Thy presence.

⟨⟩

Lock the eyelid doors and shut out the wild dance of tempting scenes. Drop your mind into the bottomless well of your heart. Hold your mind on your heart, bubbling with your life-giving blood. Keep your attention tied to the heart, until you feel its rhythmic beat. With every heartbeat, feel the knock of almighty Life. Picture the same all-pervading Life knocking at the heart-door of all human beings and all living creatures.

The heart throb constantly, meekly, announces the infinite power standing behind the doors of your awareness. The gentle beat of all-pervading Life says to you silently, "Do not receive only a little flow of My life, but expand the opening of thy feeling powers, and let Me flood thy blood, body, mind, feelings, and soul with My throbs of universal life."

Breathlessness Is Deathlessness

Breath is life. If you can live without breathing, you will prolong your life and rise above body-consciousness to Soul-consciousness while still living in your physical body. To be truly breathless doesn't come about by suppressing the breath or holding it forcibly in the lungs. Rather, breathlessness lifts one to a state of inner calmness and relaxation, making it simply unnecessary for you to breathe for a time.

You can practice this technique at any time. Wherever you are, sit erect with your spine straight, and deeply relax. Close your eyes (or fix their gaze, eyes half closed, at the point between the eyebrows). Now, with deep calmness, mentally watch your breath, *without controlling it, as it enters and exits the body*. As the breath enters, move the index finger of your right hand inward, toward the thumb, and mentally (without moving your tongue or lips) chant "*Hong*." As the breath exits, straighten the index finger, and mentally chant "*Sau*" (pronounced "saw"). (The purpose for moving the index finger is to become more positive in your concentration, and to differentiate the inhalation from the exhalation.)

Do not in any way control the breath mentally. Assume, rather, the calm attitude of a *silent observer,* watching the breath's natural flow as it enters and exits the body—a flow of which you are generally not particularly aware.

Practice this technique with great reverence and attention for at least ten minutes (to begin with). The longer your practice, the better. You can practice it at any time, day or night, during formal meditation or in your leisure time—for instance, while riding in a car (provided you aren't driving!), or even while lying on your back in bed. It will give you a deep sense of inner calmness, and will bring you at last to the realization that you are not the body, but the soul— superior to and independent of this material body.

For formal meditation, sit on a straight-backed, armless chair. Place a woolen blanket over the chair, covering the back and letting it run down beneath your feet. Face east. Sit erect, away from the back of the chair.

The *Hong Sau* technique can also be practiced, as I said, during leisure moments—such as sitting in a doctor's waiting room. Simply watch the breath, and as you do so, mentally chant "*Hong*" and "*Sau*," without moving the finger, closing the eyes, or gazing upward at the point between the eyebrows, or doing anything that might attract the attention of others around you. Keep your eyes open, if you like, without blinking, perhaps looking straight ahead, or at some particular point. Keep the spine erect, if possible, and if you can do so unobtrusively.

The purpose of the *Hong Sau* technique is to help you to free your attention from outwardness, and to withdraw it from the senses, for breath is the cord that keeps the soul tied to the body. Man lives in an atmosphere of air, which he requires even as a fish requires water. By rising above the breath in breathlessness, man can enter the celestial realms of light, where the angels dwell. By dispassionately watching the breath coming in and going out, one's breathing naturally slows, calming at last the peace-disturbing activity of the heart, lungs, and diaphragm.

Consider for a moment this extraordinary fact: The heart normally pumps about twelve tons of blood a day! It gets no rest even at night, when most of the other organs have a chance to suspend their activity at least partially. The most worked (and overworked) organ in the body is the heart. The *Hong Sau* technique is a scientific method for resting the heart, increasing longevity thereby, and liberating a vast amount of Life Current, or energy, to be distributed over the whole body, renewing all the body cells and preventing their decay.

This marvelous, though simple, technique is one of India's greatest contributions to the world. It lengthens man's lifespan, and is a practical method for rising above body-consciousness and realizing oneself as the Immortal Spirit. The words, *Hong* and *Sau*, are a Sanskrit saying, given mantric power. The basic saying, *Aham saha*, means, "I—am He."

The Importance of Relaxation

In sleep, we experience sensory relaxation. Death is complete, though involuntary, relaxation of the spirit from the body. It comes after the arrest of the heart's action. By the *"Hong Sau"* technique, one can reach the point of even relaxing the heart, and thereby rising above its compulsion to outwardness, experiencing death *consciously*, and eliminating one sense of the mystery of death and the fear of dying. One can learn, indeed, to leave his body voluntarily and blissfully, instead of being thrown out of it forcefully, often as a complete surprise, at death.

Inattention during practice of this technique can be soporific, producing sleep. Concentrated attention, on the other hand, brings to every body cell a tingling sense of divine life.

If you have the time, practice the technique longer—indeed, as long as you like. I myself, as a boy, used to practice it for seven hours at a time, and thereby achieved a deep state of breathless trance. Hold to the great calmness you feel during and after this practice. Cling to that peace as long as possible. Apply it in practical life situations, when dealing with people, when studying, when doing business, when thinking. And use it to help you to practice self-control, when trying to rid yourself of some deep-seated, harmful mental or emotional habit. Whenever a situation demands it, recall to mind the calmness you've felt during and after the practice of this technique, and, reliving that state, meet the situation from that calm inner center, where your natural soul-intuition will ensure the best possible outcome.

Remember, deep intensity of concentration is necessary for the correct practice of this technique. This does not mean, however, that there should be any sense of strain present. Practice the technique calmly, with relaxation—even with reverence—and feel in that calmness that you are placing yourself in readiness to listen to, and to become absorbed in, the Cosmic Vibration, AUM. *Hong Sau* will help to put you in contact with the Great Spirit, who is present in you as your soul, and whose expression is vibration, the cause of that inner sound. Results will positively come, and deep calmness will be yours. Higher intuitions will come to you after prolonged practice, and you will find yourself in touch with the unexplored reservoir of divine power.

Do not be impatient. Keep on steadily. Incorporate this practice into your regular routine, making it as much a part of your day as eating, brushing your teeth and bathing, or sleeping. Supremely beneficial effects will pervade your whole mental and physical constitution.

As in everything else, the highest results cannot be attained in a day or even in days. Practice! Practice the technique, and apply to your daily needs the calmness it produces. Remember also, I speak from experience—not only my own, but that of centuries of experience by the great yogis in my country. You, too, can have the same glorious experience as they, if you persevere in your practice.

Final, Important Point: Where to Concentrate?

Where should you focus your attention, while practicing this technique? On the breath, yes, but w*here* in the body?

Your attention, at first, may be on the pumping lungs and diaphragm. Concentrate first, then, on that physical movement. Gradually, as the mind grows calm, shift your attention from the body to the breath itself. Be aware of the breath where it enters the body, in the nostrils. As you grow calmer still, try to feel where, in the nostrils, the flow is strongest. At first it will be at the outer nostrils themselves, but as your concentration deepens try to feel the breath higher in the nose, and note where the flow seems strongest. Is it in the upper part of the nose? the sides? the bottom? This can even help you to perceive more clearly your own state of mind. In the upper part, the flow may indicate a higher awareness. In the lower, a certain downward flow of energy in the spine. On the outer sides of the nostrils, the flow may reflect a tendency somewhat to react emotionally. Toward the center of the nostrils, there may be a tendency toward withdrawal. As you grow still calmer, feel the breath where it enters the head, up by the point between the eyebrows—the actual seat of concentration in the body.

The origin of the breath lies in the astral body. Astral inhalation corresponds to an upward movement through what is known in the Yoga teachings as *iḍa*. Astral exhalation corresponds to a downward movement through the *pingala* nerve channel. These channels may be observed by those who eat fish as the two little nerves that run down the length of the spine.

An upward flow of energy through *iḍa* accompanies inhalation of the physical breath. And a downward flow through *pingala* accompanies physical exhalation. Astral breathing is accomplished by this upward and downward movement of energy. It is intrinsic to the reactive process. When the upward flow of energy is stronger, a positive reaction is indicated, and the same is true with deliberate physical inhalation. When the movement is more strongly downward (or when the physical exhalation is stronger than the inhalation), it comes out as a sigh, and indicates a feeling of rejection. When the inhalation is longer than the exhalation, it is an indication of positive reaction—even one of excitement. When the exhalation is longer, there is a corresponding withdrawal into oneself. In sleep, the exhalation is twice as long as the inhalation. When inhalation and exhalation are equal in duration, there is inner equanimity.

※

Don't waste the perception of God's presence, acquired in meditation, by useless chatting. Idle words are like bullets: they riddle the milk pail of peace. In devoting time unnecessarily to conversation and exuberant laughter, you'll find you have nothing left inside. Fill the pail of your consciousness with the milk of meditative peace, then keep it filled. Joking is false happiness. Too much laughter riddles the mind and lets the peace in the bucket flow out, wasting it.

※

Intuition is that faculty of the soul which at once directly perceives the truth about anything. Without the power of intuition, you cannot know Truth. Intuition means "soul-perception," and is the knowing power of the soul, without the help of the senses or the mind. Intuition can give you knowledge about things that your senses and understanding can never give.

Many books and courses of study are prescribed for students in school, but nothing is taught about concentration and the development of the sixth sense, the all-knowing faculty of intuition. Many people make mistakes in everything, from health and business to philosophy and religion. Thousands of people make wrong investments and take wrong paths because their minds are not scientifically guided by intuition.

By the development of intuition one can outgrow the law of cause and effect in one's own life. Intuition tunes the mental radio so that it can intercept all vibrations of future happenings, which otherwise are deflected by diverse currents.

Pure reason and calm feeling lead to intuition. Therefore, the first requisite in developing it is to calmly reason and calmly feel everything. Intuition is developed by exercising common sense, daily introspection and analysis, depth of thought and continued activity in one direction, calmness, and, best of all, by holding on to the calm after-effects of meditation.

If you can produce a perfect state of calmness in concentration and meditation, you will be able to solve deep problems. If you hold onto the calmness that comes after meditation, then you will be guided aright. Intuition guides your reason. When you have developed intuition, you will stand firm in your knowledge, though the universe rise up to defeat you. Whenever you want to solve a problem intuitively, first go into deep meditation or silence. Do not think of your problem during meditation, but meditate until you feel a sense of calmness filling the inner recesses of your body, and your breath becomes calm and quiet. Then ask God to direct your intuition so that you may know what you should do.

First, seek the truth about simple problems; then, when your intuition is working infallibly, use it to find solutions to big problems. For example, suppose two propositions are given to you about a business matter; both propositions seem attractive, but both cannot be right for you. You must decide between them, and you can decide rightly by your intuitive sense. Supermen continually use their intuition in everything they do, and thus accomplish the seemingly impossible.

You who are reading, and I who am writing, and all the two billion people throbbing with life today,* will exist a hundred years hence only as thoughts. Great and small must be buried beneath the grass or thrown into the hungry flames of cremation. We, who are so sure of our breakfasts, lunches, and dinners, will be unable to swallow or to speak. Our lips will be sealed forever.

If each and every soul's cheap garment of flesh must be discarded that the soul may put on the shining raiment of immortality, why should you cry? If immortality-declaring saints and trembling-at-death small men must die, then why fear death? It is a universal experience through which all must pass.

Why spend all the treasure of your wisdom trying to make this uncertain, perishable body comfortable? Wake up! Try to reap the harvest of imperishable immortality and lasting, ever-new bliss on the perishable soil of the body. You will never find lasting comfort from a slowly diminishing body. You can never squeeze the honey of divine happiness from the rock of sense pleasures.

Lasting comfort flows ceaselessly into the pail of your life when you squeeze the honeycomb of meditation and

* Written in 1934.

peace with the eager, powerful hands of will, and with ever-deeper concentration.

I do not mean that you should be a cynic and not enjoy the things of this life. All I say is, do not be so attached to anything that you will feel mental agony when you forcibly are separated from it. If you do not grieve for earthly things when your bodily garment is cast off, you will have better things hereafter. You will again receive from the hands of your Father, God, all the things that you ever cherished and lost. He takes things from you so that you will not remain earthbound and forgetful of your true immortal state.

Acquire the power of meditation and the treasures of intuitional perceptions and ever-new peace and joy, which will be of the greatest use to you on your last journey. Forget the delusions of today. Get ready for death by making your acquaintance with God every day. At the end of the trail, through the portals of that last day, you will be allowed entry into the Kingdom of your Father, and will remain there forever.

CHAPTER *8*

YOUR ALL-POWERFUL DIVINE NATURE

The Lion Who Became a Sheep

A lioness, huge with an unborn baby lion in her body, was growing weak from lack of food. As the baby lion grew heavier within her, she could not move quickly enough to catch any prey.

Roaring with sadness and hunger, and heavy with the baby lion, the lioness fell asleep at the edge of the forest near a pasture. As she dozed, she dreamt of seeing a flock of sheep grazing. When, in her dream, she pounced on one of the sheep, she jerked herself awake. With surprise and great joy, she discovered that her dream was true: a large flock of sheep grazed in the pasture right near her.

Forgetting the heavy baby lion in her body, and impelled by the madness of hunger, the lioness pounced on one of the young lambs and took it into the depths of the forest. The lioness did not realize that during the exertion of her mad leap at the lamb she had given birth to the baby lion.

The flock of sheep were so paralyzed with fear by the attack of the lioness that they couldn't run away. When the lioness had departed and the panic was over, the sheep woke from their stupor. They began to bleat out lamentations for their lost comrade, when, to their great astonishment, they discovered the helpless baby lion crooning in their midst.

One of the mother sheep took pity on the baby lion and adopted it as her own.

The young lion grew up amidst the flock of sheep. Several years passed, and there, with a flock of sheep, roamed a huge lion with long mane and tail, behaving exactly like a sheep. The sheep-lion bleated instead of roaring and ate grass instead of meat. This vegetarian lion acted exactly like a weak, meek lamb.

One day, another lion strolled out of the nearby forest onto the green pasture, and to his great delight beheld this flock of sheep. Thrilled with joy and whipped by hunger, the great lion pursued the fleeing flock of sheep, when, with amazement, he saw a huge lion, with tail high up in the air, fleeing at top speed ahead of the sheep.

The older lion paused for a moment, scratched his head, and pondered within himself: "I can understand the sheep flying away from me, but I cannot imagine why this stalwart lion should run at the sight of me. This runaway lion interests me." Ignoring his hunger, he raced hard and pounced upon the escaping lion. The sheep-lion fainted with fear. The big lion was puzzled more than ever, and slapped the sheep-lion out of his swoon. In a deep voice he rebuked, "What's the matter with you?! Why do you, my brother, flee from me?"

The sheep-lion closed his eyes and bleated out in sheep language, "Please let me go. Don't kill me. I'm just a sheep brought up with yonder flock."

"Oh, now I see why you're bleating." The big lion pondered again, and a great idea flashed upon him. He caught the sheep-lion by the mane with his mighty jaws and dragged him toward a lake at the end of the pasture. When the big lion reached the shore of the lake, he pushed the sheep-lion's head so that it was reflected in the water. He began to shake the sheep-lion, who still had his eyes tightly closed, saying, "Open your eyes! Look! You are not a sheep."

"Bleat, bleat, bleat. Please don't kill me. Let me go. I am not a lion, but only a poor, meek sheep," wailed the sheep-lion.

The big lion gave the sheep-lion a terrible shake. The sheep-lion opened his eyes, and was astonished to find the reflection of his head was not a sheep's head as he expected, but a lion's head, like that of the one who was shaking him with his paw. Then the big lion said: "Look at my face and your face reflected in the water. They are the same. My face roars. Now! You must roar instead of bleating."

The sheep-lion, convinced, tried to roar, but could only produce bleat-mingled roars. As the older lion continued to exhort him with slapping paws, the sheep-lion at last succeeded in roaring. Then both of the lions bounded across the pasture, and returned to live in the den of lions.

The above story aptly illustrates how most of us, though made in the all-powerful image of the Divine Lion of the Universe, have been born and brought up in the sheepfold of mortal weakness. We bleat with fear, lack, and death, instead of roaring with immortality and power, and preying on wisdom and unlimited prosperity.

These teachings are the new lion that will drag you to the crystal pool of meditation and give you such a hard shaking that you will open the closed eyes of your wisdom and behold yourself as the Lion of Divinity, made in the image of the Cosmic Lion. Those of you who strive continuously will forget your mortal fears of weakness, failure, and death, and will learn to roar with the power of almighty immortality.

◈

Being endowed with free choice, I am in reality the son of God. I have been dreaming that I am a mortal man. I am now awake. The dream of my soul imprisoned in my bodily cage has vanished. I am everything that my Heavenly Father is.

◈

The person who finds God owns the cosmos and everything in it. Jesus knew that He was one with the Father. That is why he could do things that other mortals could not do. So, spend your time in daily meditation, longer and deeper, which is the quickest way to become Christlike. Striving for God-contact in meditation is pure joy. You will be happy when you meditate, and you will be happier still when you arrive at the end of the trail of meditation and meet God, the King of ever-new happiness.

When Jesus said, "Foxes have holes, and birds of the air have nests, but the son of man hath nowhere to lay his head," he was not bemoaning his poverty. Instead, he was saying that he was the owner of the cosmos, because he did not remain caged in a small place as earthly creatures do. Jesus also said, "Bread, the men of the world seek after (matter-loving, short-sighted persons), but seek ye first the Kingdom of God (the entire cosmos), and all these things (prosperity, wisdom, happiness) shall be added unto you (without your asking)."

This earth is a place of mirth, a pleasure house for immortals. Because we forget this and become identified with the earthly play, we suffer. We must remember that our real home is the mansion of changeless, ever-new, blissful, omnipresent immortality. We are eternally God's children, whether naughty or good, but when we forget that our home is God's kingdom and get mixed up with the earthly show, we make ourselves miserable. We must learn that we are immortal, made in God's blissful image.

There is one thing you will never tire of, either in this life or throughout eternity, and that is the ever-new joy realized in God-contact. Joy that is always the same may cause boredom, but joy that is ever-new will last forever. Such joy can be found only in deep meditation.

Fostering the desire for luxuries is the surest way to increase misery. Don't be the slave of things or possessions; boil down even your "needs." Spend your time in search of lasting happiness or bliss. The unchangeable, immortal soul is hidden behind the screen of your consciousness on which are painted disease, failure, and death. Lift the veil of illusive change, and become established in your immortal nature. Enthrone your fickle consciousness on the changelessness and calmness within you, which is the throne of God; then, let your soul manifest bliss night and day.

The soul's nature is bliss—a lasting inner state of ever-new, ever-changing joy, which eternally entertains without changing the one entertained even when he passes through the trials of physical suffering or death.

Desirelessness is not negation; rather, it is the attainment of the self-control you need in order to regain the eternal heritage of all-fulfillment within your soul. First, by meditation, give the soul the opportunity to manifest this state, and then, constantly living in this state, do your duty to your body and mind, and to the world. You need not give up your ambitions and become negative; on the contrary, let the ever-lasting joy, which is your real nature, help you to realize all noble ambitions. Enjoy noble experiences with the joy of God. Perform real duties with divine joy.

You are all gods, if you only knew it. Behind the wave of your consciousness is the sea of God's presence. You must look within. Don't look at the little wave of the body with its weaknesses, but look beneath it. Close your eyes and see only the vast omnipresence before you, everywhere you look. You are in the center of that vast sphere, and you will find it is filled with the great bliss that lights the stars, and gives power to the winds and storms. God is the fountain of all our joys and of all manifestations in nature.

God has not to be earned. "Seek ye first the kingdom of God, and all these things shall be added unto you. Nor be ye of doubtful mind." Awaken yourself from the gloom of ignorance. Awake, and you shall behold the glory of God—the vast vista of God's light spreading over all things. I am telling you to be divine realists, and you will find the answer to all questions in God.

Meditation is the only way. Beliefs and reading books cannot give you realization. It is only by meditating in the right way that you can have that great realization and joy. If you practice this, you will know that God cannot be moved by blind prayer and flattery, but He *can* be moved by law and devotion, and by the love of your heart.

Surrender yourself to God. You must claim your Divine Birthright. Your constant prayer, your boundless determination, and your constant desire for God will make Him break his tremendous vow of silence, and He will answer you. In the temple of silence He will give you the gift of Himself, which will last beyond the portals of the tomb.

When you see a motion picture of a stage performance and you already know the play beforehand, the movie will not be so interesting. It is good that you don't understand this life, because God is playing a motion picture in your life. If you knew what was going to happen, it wouldn't be interesting. Don't be worried about the ending, but always pray to God, "Teach me to play my part in this drama of life — weak or strong, sick or well, rich or poor — with an attitude of immortality, that at the end of this drama I may know the moral of it all."

Do not waste your time. You are God's greatest creation. We are blessed that we can think. God says, "I gave you will. I gave you freedom and free choice. Perhaps you will forsake all things and love Me who gave those gifts to you."

I have found all the silver streamlets of my desire leading to that great Ocean of Consciousness. If you keep on following the good in life, you will flow down the river of desire into the ocean of God's consciousness. All the material realities that challenge you will be unreal. Today we are and tomorrow we are not, but we must remember our utmost duty to that great Power which is behind all our lives. In acting the drama of our lives we must remember our highest duty to Him.

If you want to understand this life, you must remember the delicate work He is doing in the flowers, the flame of His mind that is burning in our thoughts, the thoughts that are pouring from our souls, and the worlds upon worlds that are spread out over the vastness of the cosmos. How vast is that God, and yet we can feel Him in our consciousness. Our lives are a reflection of that Spirit. No life can exist without the ocean of life behind it; we must realize that great ocean of life throbbing behind our lives.

⚬

The habit of beholding yourself as the little body in the small playhouse of the world must be displaced by God habits. Human habits remind you of the little, unreal happiness of name, fame, and laughably valueless possessions. Possess the Universe, for the whole Universe is yours, O Prince of all Possessions! Forsake the slums of the beggar-ego, O Prince-Image of God! Never mind what length of time you have spent and must still spend identified with matter. All of the ages past are as nothing compared to the eternity of time before you, which you may spend in the bosom of God, in the full and conscious possession of all His Glory. No matter how long you have erred and run away from God, you may now forsake the no-longer-attractive slums of ego and reclaim your kingdom of divine bliss in eternity.

The little centuries of human years are but days, nay, but a few hours, in God's consciousness. Awake from dreams of littleness to the realization of the vastness within you. You are dreaming you are a bumblebee, buzzing around the poisoned honey of blossoming sense-lures. Come! I will show you, my beloved, that God is honeycombed in everything. Drink Him through all noble experiences.

No longer feed your human habits with delusive human actions. Let them slowly starve for want of the food of activity. Come! Meditate daily, with earnestness and devotion. Love God without ceasing. Thus may your omnipresent nature be revived in your consciousness, displacing body-bound, sense-limited human beliefs and habits.

Drink the nectar of God-love in all hearts. Use every heart as your own wine cup from which to drink the fresh ambrosia of God-love. Drink not this divine love from one heart only, but drink freely from all hearts the love of God alone.

Learn to love God as the joy felt in meditation. Victory is very near. Choose only good paths before you start the race to the goal of realization. Think of God as you start on the path of your material or spiritual duty. Then think of God with each footfall of your advancing feet as you make your way carefully and joyously over the broadening road of fulfillment. Ask God to be with you when you, by your own will, choose good action. Think of God before you eat body-nourishing food; think of Him while you are eating it. Then, when you are finished eating, think of God.

When you act in the world forgetting God, you have changed your center from God to matter. This material nature will throw you into the whirlpool of change and will stifle you with worries and sorrows. Revert to your own, true nature. Change your center from material desires to desire for God. Remember God as peace and bliss in your heart always. Ask God to make your peace, silence, joy, and meditation his holy altars, where your soul may meet and commune with Him. Let your prayer be: "Make my understanding the temple of Thy guidance!"

Invoke God as power in the temple of consciousness during the day. Let every action and every word that you utter be tinged and tipsy with God-love intoxication. Talk and act sensibly, as a man who drinks a lot and yet remains in command. Be drunk with God, and let every action of your daily life be a temple of God's memory. Perform every action to please Him; and in the indestructible shrine of your devotion God will listen to every thought.

Carry your love of God deep in your heart before you sleep. Cradle it there, so that when you dream you may dream of Him resting on the fragrant altar of sleep. Actually, God embraces you on His bosom as peace and joy when you sleep. You are sleeping locked in His arms of tranquility.

So, before you fall asleep, remember that you are going to embrace Him in sleep and dreams.

And when you are deeply sleeping or meditating, feel Him embracing you as the Omnipresent Bliss. Through His bliss-touch He wants to make you forget your little, painful memories, mental and physical aches, and spiritual agonies, which you garnered during your truant stay in the slums of matter.

Enthrone peace and joy in your heart. Feel that joy, no matter what you do. If you can do this, though the universe explode into nothingness or your body be torn by trials, you will find Him dancing in your memory forever and forever. Let pure joy dance in your memory, and God will dance with you.

Hold fast to your once-lost spiritual treasure of joy. Now that it is regained, increase it by giving it freely to others. Remember that whatever we selfishly keep for self is lost; and whatever we freely give in love to others yields an ever-increasing harvest of happiness. Worry and selfishness are highwaymen on the roads of life; they hold us up and rob us of our joy and peace. So, determine to hold fast to joy, even if your mind tells you that "all is lost." Drown all confusing noises in the silent, sweet harmony of your perfect, invincible joy.

Enthrone joy in the sanctuary of all your aspirations, noble actions, and noble thoughts. Then you will feel God as joy reigning in the kingdom of your soul, laying His scepter on the white altar of your dreams to make every thought, feeling, and memory a flower blooming there.

Remember this, my beloved: With Her veil of sleep and peace, Divine Mother wipes away the dark sorrows of her ignorance-besmirched children. Go then to your dreams as a child to its mother's arms. Divine love will be enshrined in all your memories of past incarnations and present thoughts. Then you will find that evil and misery were only your own imaginary dream-creations. You slept and dreamt a nightmare of evil; you awake in God and feel only joy and good existing everywhere.

And, when the divine memory of constant joy shall arise on the Resurrection Day of your soul's return to its inheritance, you will forget forever your self-created nightmares of evil and will behold with clear eyes the perfect beauty and goodness that exists everywhere, because God is everywhere.

Then you will pray the only prayer that I pray for myself: "Heavenly Father, may Thy love shine forever on the shrine of my devotion. May my devotion for Thee forever burn on the altar of my memory, and may I be able to kindle love for Thee on all altar-hearts."

INDEX

Index

About the Author

PARAMHANSA YOGANANDA

"As a bright light shining in the midst of darkness, so was Yogananda's presence in this world. Such a great soul comes on earth only rarely, when there is a real need among men."

—The Shankaracharya of Kanchipuram

Born in India in 1893, Paramhansa Yogananda was trained from his early years to bring India's ancient science of Self-realization to the West. In 1920 he moved to the United States to begin what was to develop into a worldwide work touching millions of lives. Americans were hungry for India's spiritual teachings, and for the liberating techniques of yoga.

In 1946 he published what has become a spiritual classic and one of the best-loved books of the twentieth century, *Autobiography of a Yogi*. In addition, Yogananda established headquarters for a worldwide work, wrote a number of books and study courses, gave lectures to thousands in most major cities across the United States, wrote music and poetry, and trained disciples. He was invited to the White House by Calvin Coolidge, and he initiated Mahatma Gandhi into Kriya Yoga, his most advanced meditation technique.

Yogananda's message to the West highlighted the unity of all religions, and the importance of love for God combined with scientific techniques of meditation.

FURTHER EXPLORATIONS

The original 1946 unedited edition of Yogananda's spiritual masterpiece

AUTOBIOGRAPHY OF A YOGI
by Paramhansa Yogananda

Autobiography of a Yogi is one of the best-selling Eastern philosophy titles of all time, with millions of copies sold, named one of the best and most influential books of the twentieth century. This highly prized reprinting of the original 1946 edition is the only one available free from textual changes made after Yogananda's death. Yogananda was the first yoga master of India whose mission was to live and teach in the West.

In this updated edition are bonus materials, including a last chapter that Yogananda wrote in 1951, without posthumous changes. This new edition also includes the eulogy that Yogananda wrote for Gandhi, and a new foreword and afterword by Swami Kriyananda, one of Yogananda's close, direct disciples.

This edition of *Autobiography of a Yogi* is also available in unabridged audiobook (MP3) format, read by Swami Kriyananda, Yogananda's direct disciple.

Praise for Autobiography of a Yogi

"In the original edition, published during Yogananda's life, one is more in contact with Yogananda himself. While Yogananda founded centers and organizations, his concern was more with guiding individuals to direct communion with Divinity rather than with promoting any one church as opposed to another. This spirit is easier to grasp in the original edition of this great spiritual and yogic classic."

— **David Frawley**, Director, American Institute of Vedic Studies,
author of *Yoga and Ayurveda*

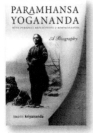

PARAMHANSA YOGANANDA
A Biography with Personal Reflections and Reminiscences
by Swami Kriyananda

Paramhansa Yogananda's classic *Autobiography of a Yogi* is more about the saints Yogananda met than about himself—in spite of the fact that Yogananda was much greater than many he described. Now, one of Yogananda's few remaining direct disciples relates the untold story of this great spiritual master and world teacher: his teenage miracles, his challenges in coming to America, his national lecture campaigns, his struggles to fulfill his world-changing mission amid incomprehension and painful betrayals, and his ultimate triumphant achievement. Kriyananda's subtle grasp of his guru's inner nature reveals Yogananda's many-sided greatness. Includes many never-before-published anecdotes.

THE NEW PATH
My Life with Paramhansa Yogananda
by Swami Kriyananda

This is the moving story of Kriyananda's years with Paramhansa Yogananda, India's emissary to the West and the first yoga master to spend the greater part of his life in America. When Swami Kriyananda discovered *Autobiography of a Yogi* in 1948, he was totally new to Eastern teachings. This is a great advantage to the Western reader, since Kriyananda walks us along the yogic path as he discovers it from the moment of his initiation as a disciple of Yogananda. With winning honesty, humor, and deep insight, he shares his journey on the spiritual path through personal stories and experiences. Through more than four hundred stories of life with Yogananda, we tune in more deeply to this great master and to the teachings he brought to the West. This book is an ideal complement to *Autobiography of a Yogi*.

TWO SOULS: FOUR LIVES
The Lives and Former Lives of Paramhansa Yogananda
and his disciple, Swami Kriyananda
Catherine Kairavi

This book explores an astonishing statement made by
Paramhansa Yogananda, that he was the historical figure,
William the Conqueror, in a previous incarnation.

The Norman Conquest of England was one of the pivotal
moments in world history, a series of events that affects us even today. Is it
possible that two of the greatest men of that era—William the Conqueror
and his son, Henry I of England—have recently reincarnated as the great
spiritual master Paramhansa Yogananda (author of the classic *Autobiography
of a Yogi*) and his close disciple, Swami Kriyananda? If so, what are the subtle
connections between the Norman Conquest and modern times?

THE ESSENCE OF THE BHAGAVAD GITA
Explained by Paramhansa Yogananda
As Remembered by his disciple, Swami Kriyananda

Rarely in a lifetime does a new spiritual classic appear that
has the power to change people's lives and transform future
generations. This is such a book. This revelation of India's
best-loved scripture approaches it from a fresh perspective,
showing its deep allegorical meaning and its down-to-earth
practicality. The themes presented are universal: how to achieve victory in life
in union with the divine; how to prepare for life's "final exam," death, and what
happens afterward; how to triumph over all pain and suffering.

"A brilliant text that will greatly enhance the spiritual life of every reader."
        —**Caroline Myss**, author of *Anatomy of the Spirit* and *Sacred Contracts*

*"It is doubtful that there has been a more important spiritual writing in the last fifty
years than this soul-stirring, monumental work. What a gift! What a treasure!"*
        —**Neale Donald Walsch**, author of *Conversations with God*

REVELATIONS OF CHRIST

Proclaimed by Paramhansa Yogananda
Presented by his disciple, Swami Kriyananda

The rising tide of alternative beliefs proves that now, more than ever, people are yearning for a clear-minded and uplifting understanding of the life and teachings of Jesus Christ. This galvanizing book, presenting the teachings of Christ from the experience and perspective of Paramhansa Yogananda, one of the greatest spiritual masters of the twentieth century, finally offers the fresh perspective on Christ's teachings for which the world has been waiting. *Revelations of Christ* presents us with an opportunity to understand and apply the scriptures in a more reliable way than any other: by studying under those saints who have communed directly, in deep ecstasy, with Christ and God.

"This is a great gift to humanity. It is a spiritual treasure to cherish and to pass on to children for generations."

—**Neale Donald Walsch**, author of *Conversations with God*

"Kriyananda's revelatory book gives us the enlightened, timeless wisdom of Jesus the Christ in a way that addresses the challenges of twenty-first century living."

—**Michael Beckwith**, Founder and Spiritual Director, Agape International Spiritual Center, author of *Inspirations of the Heart*

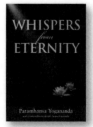

WHISPERS FROM ETERNITY

Paramhansa Yogananda,
Edited by his disciple Swami Kriyananda

Many poetic works can inspire, but few, like this one, have the power to change your life. Yogananda was not only a spiritual master, but a master poet, whose verses revealed the hidden divine presence behind even everyday things. This book has the power to rapidly accelerate your spiritual growth, and provides hundreds of delightful ways for you to begin your own conversation with God.

CONVERSATIONS WITH YOGANANDA
Recorded, Compiled, and Edited with commentary by his disciple, Swami Kriyananda

This is an unparalleled, first-hand account of the teachings of Paramhansa Yogananda. Featuring nearly 500 never-before-released stories, sayings, and insights, this is an extensive, yet eminently accessible treasure trove of wisdom from one of the 20th Century's most famous yoga masters.

"A wonderful book! To find a previously unknown message from Yogananda now is an extraordinary spiritual gift. Open up at random for an encouraging word from one of the century's most beloved spiritual teachers."

— **Neale Donald Walsch**, author of *Conversations with God*

THE ESSENCE OF SELF-REALIZATION
The Wisdom of Paramhansa Yogananda
Recorded, Compiled, and Edited
by his disciple Swami Kriyananda

"With nearly three hundred of Paramhansa Yogananda's sayings rich with spiritual wisdom, this book is the fruit of a labor of love by his disciple, Swami Kriyananda. A glance at the table of contents will convince the reader of the vast scope of this book. It offers as complete an explanation of life's true purpose, and of the way to achieve that purpose, as may be found anywhere.

~ The WISDOM of YOGANANDA series ~

Six volumes of Paramhansa Yogananda's timeless wisdom in an approachable, easy-to-read format. The writings of the Master are presented with minimal editing, to capture his expansive and compassionate wisdom, his sense of fun, and his practical spiritual guidance.

HOW TO BE HAPPY ALL THE TIME
The Wisdom of Yogananda Series, VOLUME 1

Yogananda powerfully explains virtually everything needed to lead a happier, more fulfilling life. Topics include: looking for happiness in the right places; choosing to be happy; tools and techniques for achieving happiness; sharing happiness with others; balancing success and happiness; and many more.

KARMA & REINCARNATION
The Wisdom of Yogananda Series, VOLUME 2

Yogananda reveals the truth behind karma, death, reincarnation, and the afterlife. With clarity and simplicity, he makes the mysterious understandable. Topics include: why we see a world of suffering and inequality; how to handle the challenges in our lives; what happens at death, and after death; and the purpose of reincarnation.

SPIRITUAL RELATIONSHIPS
The Wisdom of Yogananda Series, VOLUME 3

This book contains practical guidance and fresh insight on relationships of all types. Topics include: how to cure bad habits that can end true friendship; how to choose the right partner; sex in marriage and how to conceive a spiritual child; problems that arise in marriage; the Universal Love behind all your relationships.

HOW TO BE A SUCCESS
The Wisdom of Yogananda Series, VOLUME 4

This book includes the complete text of *The Attributes of Success,* the original booklet later published as *The Law of Success.* In addition, you will learn how to find your purpose in life, develop habits of success and eradicate habits of failure, develop your will power and magnetism, and thrive in the right job.

HOW TO ACHIEVE GLOWING HEALTH & VITALITY
The Wisdom of Yogananda Series, volume 6

Paramhansa Yogananda, a foremost spiritual teacher of modern times, offers practical, wide-ranging, and fascinating suggestions on how to have more energy and live a radiantly healthy life. The principles in this book promote physical health and all-round well-being, mental clarity, and ease and inspiration in your spiritual life. Readers will discover the priceless Energization Exercises for rejuvenating the body and mind, the fine art of conscious relaxation, and helpful diet tips for health and beauty.

THE RUBAIYAT OF OMAR KHAYYAM EXPLAINED
Paramhansa Yogananda,
Edited by his disciple Swami Kriyananda

The Rubaiyat is loved by Westerners as a hymn of praise to sensual delights. In the East its quatrains are considered a deep allegory of the soul's romance with God, based solely on the author Omar Khayyam's reputation as a sage and mystic. But for centuries the meaning of this famous poem has remained a mystery. Now Yogananda reveals the secret meaning and the golden spiritual treasures hidden behind the Rubaiyat's verses, and presents a new scripture to the world.

THE BHAGAVAD GITA
According to Paramhansa Yogananda
Edited by Swami Kriyananda

This translation of the Gita, by Paramhansa Yoga-nanda, brings alive the deep spiritual insights and poetic beauty of the famous battlefield dialogue between Krishna and Arjuna. Based on the little-known truth that each character in the Gita represents an aspect of our own being, it expresses with revelatory clarity how to win the struggle within between the forces of our lower and higher natures.

GOD IS FOR EVERYONE
Inspired by Paramhansa Yogananda by Swami Kriyananda

This book presents a concept of God and spiritual meaning that will broadly appeal to everyone, from the most uncertain agnostic to the most fervent believer. Clearly and simply written, thoroughly non-sectarian and non-dogmatic in its approach, it is the perfect introduction to the spiritual path. Yogananda's core teachings are presented by his disciple, Swami Kriyananda.

AWAKEN TO SUPERCONSCIOUSNESS
by Swami Kriyananda

This popular guide includes everything you need to know about the philosophy and practice of meditation, and how to apply the meditative mind to resolve common daily conflicts in uncommon, superconscious ways. Superconsciousness is the hidden mechanism at work behind intuition, spiritual and physical healing, successful problem solving, and finding deep and lasting joy.

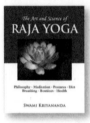

THE ART & SCIENCE OF RAJA YOGA
by Swami Kriyananda

Contains fourteen lessons in which the original yoga science emerges in all its glory—a proven system for realizing one's spiritual destiny. This is the most comprehensive course available on yoga and meditation today. Over 450 pages of text and photos give you a complete and detailed presentation of yoga postures, yoga philosophy, affirmations, meditation instruction, and breathing techniques. Also included are suggestions for daily yoga routines, information on proper diet, recipes, and alternative healing techniques. The book also comes with an audio CD that contains: a guided yoga postures sessions, a guided meditation, and an inspiring talk on how you can use these techniques to solve many of the problems of daily life.

MEDITATION FOR STARTERS
by Swami Kriyananda

If you have wanted to learn to meditate, but never had a chance, this is the place to start. Filled with easy-to-follow instructions, beautiful guided visualizations, and answers to important questions on meditation, the book includes: what meditation is (and isn't); how to relax your body and prepare yourself for going within; and techniques for interiorizing and focusing the mind. Includes a 60-minute companion CD with guided visualization and meditation instruction.

RELIGION IN THE NEW AGE
Swami Kriyananda

Our planet has entered an "Age of Energy" that will affect us for centuries to come. We can see evidence of this all around us: in ultra-fast computers, the quickening of communication and transportation, and the shrinking of time and space. This fascinating book of essays explores how this new age will change our lives, especially our spiritual seeking. Covers a wide range of upcoming societal shifts — in leadership, relationships, and self-development — including the movement away from organized religion to inner experience.

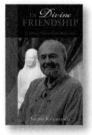

IN DIVINE FRIENDSHIP
Swami Kriyananda

This extraordinary book of nearly 250 letters, written over a thirty-year period by Swami Kriyananda, responds to practically any concern a spiritual seeker might have, such as: strengthening one's faith, accelerating one's spiritual progress, meditating more deeply, responding to illness, earning a living, attracting a mate, raising children, overcoming negative self-judgments, and responding to world upheavals.

Connecting all of these letters is the love, compassion, and wisdom of Swami Kriyananda, one of the leading spiritual figures of our time. The letters describe in detail his efforts to fulfill his Guru's commission to establish spiritual communities, and offer invaluable advice to leaders everywhere on how to avoid the temptations of materialism, selfishness, and pride. A spiritual treasure that speaks to truth seekers at all levels.

THE ART OF SUPPORTIVE LEADERSHIP
A Practical Guide for People in Positions of Responsibility

J. Donald Walters (Swami Kriyananda)

You can learn to be a more effective leader by viewing leadership in terms of shared accomplishments rather than personal advancement. Drawn from timeless Eastern wisdom, this book is clear, concise, and practical—designed from the start to produce results quickly and simply.

Used in training seminars in the U.S., Europe, and India, this book gives practical advice for leaders and potential leaders to help increase effectiveness, creativity, and team building. Individual entrepreneurs, corporations such as Kellogg, military and police personnel, and non-profit organizations are using this approach.

MONEY MAGNETISM
How to Attract What You Need When You Need It
J. Donald Walters (Swami Kriyananda)

This book can change your life by transforming how you think and feel about money. According to the author, anyone can attract wealth: "There need be no limits to the flow of your abundance." Through numerous true stories and examples, Swami Kriyananda vividly—sometimes humorously—shows you how and why the principles of money magnetism work, and how you can immediately start applying them to achieve greater success in your material and your spiritual life.

AUDIOBOOK AND MUSIC SELECTIONS

METAPHYSICAL MEDITATIONS
Swami Kriyananda

Kriyananda's soothing voice guides you in thirteen different meditations based on the soul-inspiring, mystical poetry of Paramhansa Yogananda. Each meditation is accompanied by beautiful classical music to help you quiet your thoughts and prepare for deep states of meditation. Includes a full recitation of Yogananda's poem "Samadhi," which appears in *Autobiography of a Yogi*. A great aid to the serious meditator, as well as to those just beginning their practice.

MEDITATIONS TO AWAKEN SUPERCONSCIOUSNESS
Guided Meditations on the Light
Swami Kriyananda

Featuring two beautiful guided meditations as well as an introductory section to help prepare the listener for meditation, this extraordinary recording of visualizations can be used either by itself, or as a companion to the book, *Awaken to Superconsciousness*. The soothing, transformative words, spoken over inspiring sitar background music, creates one of the most unique guided meditation products available.

RELAX: MEDITATIONS FOR FLUTE AND CELLO
Donald Walters
Featuring David Eby and Sharon Nani

This CD is specifically designed to slow respiration and heart rate, bringing listeners to their calm center. This recording features fifteen melodies for flute and cello, accompanied by harp, guitar, keyboard, and strings. Excellent for creating a calming atmosphere for work and home.

AUM: MANTRA OF ETERNITY
Swami Kriyananda

This recording features nearly seventy minutes of continuous vocal chanting of AUM, the Sanskrit word meaning peace and oneness of spirit. AUM, the cosmic creative vibration, is extensively discussed by Yogananda in *Autobiography of a Yogi*. Chanted here by his disciple, Kriyananda, this recording is a stirring way to tune into this cosmic power.

Other titles in the Mantra Series:

Gayatri Mantra*
Mahamrityanjaya Mantra*
Maha Mantra*

BLISS CHANTS
Ananda Kirtan

Chanting focuses and lifts the mind to higher states of consciousness. *Bliss Chants* features chants written by Yogananda and his direct disciple, Swami Kriyananda. They're performed by Ananda Kirtan, a group of singers and musicians from Ananda, one of the world's most respected yoga communities. Chanting is accompanied by guitar, harmonium, kirtals, and tabla.

Other titles in the Chant Series:

Divine Mother Chants	Power Chants
Love Chants	Peace Chants
Wisdom Chants*	Wellness Chants*

Visit our website to view all our available titles in books, audiobooks, spoken word, music and DVDs.

www.crystalclarity.com   * *Coming Soon*

CRYSTAL CLARITY PUBLISHERS

Crystal Clarity Publishers offers additional resources to assist you in your spiritual journey including many other books, a wide variety of inspirational and relaxation music composed by Swami Kriyananda, and yoga and meditation videos. To see a complete listing of our products, contact us for a print catalog or see our website: www.crystalclarity.com

Crystal Clarity Publishers
14618 Tyler Foote Rd., Nevada City, CA 95959
TOLL FREE: 800.424.1055 or 530.478.7600 / FAX: 530.478.7610
EMAIL: clarity@crystalclarity.com

ANANDA WORLDWIDE

Ananda Sangha, a worldwide organization founded by Swami Kriyananda, offers spiritual support and resources based on the teachings of Paramhansa Yogananda. There are Ananda spiritual communities in Nevada City, Sacramento, and Palo Alto, California; Seattle, Washington; Portland, Oregon; as well as a retreat center and European community in Assisi, Italy, and communities near New Delhi and Pune, India. Ananda supports more than 75 meditation groups worldwide.

For more information about Ananda Sangha communities or meditation groups near you, please call 530.478.7560 or visit www.ananda.org.

THE EXPANDING LIGHT

Ananda's guest retreat, The Expanding Light, offers a varied, year-round schedule of classes and workshops on yoga, meditation, and spiritual practice. You may also come for a relaxed personal renewal, participating in ongoing activities as much or as little as you wish. The beautiful serene mountain setting, supportive staff, and delicious vegetarian food provide an ideal environment for a truly meaningful, spiritual vacation.

*For more information, please call 800.346.5350
or visit www.expandinglight.org.*